T0355907

THE IMPOSSIBLE PRIZE

A Theology of Addiction

•

DONAVON RILEY

Foreword by Chad Bird

THE IMPOSSIBLE PRIZE

A Theology of Addiction

•

DONAVON RILEY

Foreword by Chad Bird

The Impossible Prize: A Theology of Addiction
© 2024 New Reformation Publications

Published by:
1517 Publishing
PO Box 54032
Irvine, CA 92619-4032

Publisher's Cataloging-In-Publication Data
(Prepared by Cassidy Cataloguing Services, Inc.)

Names: Riley, Donavon, author. | Bird, Chad, writer of foreword.
Title: The impossible prize : a theology of addiction / Donavon Riley ; foreword by Chad Bird.
Description: Irvine, CA : 1517 Publishing, [2025] | Includes bibliographical references.
Identifiers: ISBN: 978-1-962654-70-8 (paperback) | 978-1-962654-71-5 (ebook) | 978-1-962654-72-2 (audiobook)
Subjects: LCSH: Addicts—Religious life. | Compulsive behavior—Religious aspects—Christianity. | Substance abuse—Religious aspects—Christianity. | God (Christianity)—Mercy. | Christian life. | LCGFT: Self-help publications. | BISAC: SELF-HELP / Substance Abuse & Addictions / General. | RELIGION / Christian Living / Spiritual Growth. | RELIGION / Christian Living / Personal Growth.
Classification: LCC: BV4596.A24 R55 2025 | DDC: 248.8629—dc23

Printed in the United States of America.

Cover art by Zachariah James Stuef.

Table of Contents

Table of Contents

Foreword

I did not recognize him at first. A decade and a half had slipped by since we were under the same roof. In what seemed a lifetime ago, as young men, we had made midnight runs for fast food, married our respective sweethearts, and dreamed our ambitious dreams of glowing careers. Now, here we were, both in our early fifties, with gray dusting our hair and scars decorating our souls, standing face to face with each other after randomly crossing paths in an airport.

We shook hands and embraced. It had been a long time. He had an altered demeanor, a changed manner, that, at first, I could not quite put my finger on. But over the next three hours, as we talked, I knew. I had seen it before, up close and personal, in my own life and in the lives of others. A few years ago, my friend had reached the end and realized, for the first time in his life, that this was the beginning.

As it did for me, his end had come in an undoing. In a life wrecked by slavery, we pretended it was freedom. His was an addiction to one thing, mine to another, but both of us began on what we thought was a wide, pleasurable path that daily narrowed and deepened until, at the end, we were trapped in a dark, narrow, suffocating place from which there seemed no escape.

That was the end. And that was the beginning.

It was the beginning of what Donavon, with clarity and brilliance, describes in this book. The beginning of brutal honesty about human limitations and understanding that the sweet siren songs of pseudo-gods inevitably woo us into earthly hells. The beginning of finding meaning and purpose not in glorious achievements but in ongoing endurance through trials. The beginning of freedom, true and lasting freedom, not in naïve notions of human achievability but in being grasped and chosen by the unrelenting love of the God who anchors us to the cross of his Son, whose life becomes our own by grace.

Those beginnings are behind the door, which is labeled the end. This is the book that will meet you there, not as a quick-fix guide to sober living or even a roadmap to recovery, but, as Donavon calls it, "a companion—a fellow traveler on the arduous path toward understanding, acceptance, and ultimately, the embrace of a divine grace that surpasses the limits of our human striving." This fellow traveler knows the terrain, the challenges, and the setbacks. More importantly, what you will find here, and not find in most standard treatments of addiction, is a deeper, more penetrating analysis of why we are the way we are, why we do what we do, and where God is on the battlefield of our struggles to provide us with what we could never achieve on our own.

The true genius of this book is that, rather than claiming to relay novel insights, it takes us back to what is old but perennially forgotten so that it seems new. Ancient wisdom is like that. Always old, ever new, because it confronts every generation of suffering humanity with truths that, once you see them, you find it hard to believe you did not see them before. And once you see them, once they seep into the pores of your being, they fundamentally alter your view of self, the other, and of God, bringing you into conformity with life in a fallen and fractured world.

This fellow traveler introduces us to real people in the ancient text of the Bible who came to their own end and found at that conclusion a new beginning in the transformative grace of God. And though they lived millennia ago, they are just like our next-door neighbors—and just like us. They, too, tasted the bitter fruit of addiction to false gods; discovered their own powerlessness to change by a flexing of the human will; learned that struggles are where we draw nearer to God; experienced the painful but fruitful civil war that rages within us; and found, to their shock and delight, that rather than being doomed to rejection by a furious God, they were swept up into his forgiving love and anchored to a hope that defies all expectations.

Today, on the bridge between these ancient people and our lives stands Martin Luther, whose insights provide the structure and flow of this book. Though he lived and taught five hundred years ago, Luther describes the ageless reality behind our modern struggles with additions so accurately that you would think we spent hours every week baring our souls to him across a table in Germany. He knows us because he knew himself, our common human nature, and our enslaved wills. Mostly, though, Luther himself had been plucked from the abyss of despair by the hand of a merciful God, who gave him life, salvation, and hope in Jesus. And it is to Jesus that Luther leads us, that in him we too might find that we are chosen and loved by God.

For many years, I have longed for a book, *the* book that I could place in the hands of a friend, a family member, or a stranger who was wrestling with the darkness of addiction—a book that would simultaneously be readable, biblical, and theological, and would support a holistic approach to addiction. That book has now been written. It is *The Impossible Prize*. May it be for all of us who have reached the end and found it to be the beginning—a fellow traveler that recalibrates our lives to believe, fight, pray, and journey, however hesitantly, however much we fall along the way, in the only direction that leads to hope and healing—to Jesus, the friend of sinners.

Chad Bird
Scholar in Residence at 1517

"Addiction"

In the abyss of my pain, I found addiction,
A seductive mistress that straddled my weary soul.
Its fingers caress my every thought,
Dragging me deeper into its treacherous embrace.

Day by day, I smirked and winked at my destruction,
Seeking solace in the numbing haze it brought.
But beneath the surface, I could feel my spirit wither,
And the flicker of hope in me began to rot.

Then in the darkest hour, when all seemed lost,
I heard a shout amidst the chaos and wretched faces.
A firm voice that called out my name,
Promising freedom from this endless midnight.

It was Jesus who reached out His hand,
His love tearing away addiction's frigid grip.
With grace and mercy, He pulled me close,
And in His presence, I found a saving grace.

He cleansed my wounds with His healing touch,
His light exorcised the shadows, exposing my demons.
With every step, He guided me towards sobriety,
Renewing my spirit and cleansing my sin.

No longer seduced by the cold caress of addiction,
I walk a path of redemption and hope.
Through His love, I am given the strength to overcome,
rise above the struggles, and learn to live.

Though scars remain as reminders of the past,
I am held wrapped in His divine grace.
For Jesus, my Savior has set me free,
And His love remains my eternal embrace.

Donavon L Riley

Preface

In the often bleak reality of addiction, where the soul wrestles with the shadows of hopelessness, the path toward sobriety feels like a pursuit of an impossible prize, which is why this book is entitled "The Impossible Prize." The very phrase captures the paradoxical essence of this exploration—a quest for sobriety and sanity that is both unattainable to us on our own, yet profoundly transformative when it is gifted to us by God. In delving into *The Impossible Prize*, we embark on a theological odyssey, a reflection on the tangled web of addiction and the inexhaustible grace of God that transcends our human limitations.

Addiction, in its relentless grip, often distracts us with the illusion of self-sufficiency. It entices us into the deceptive game of attempting to live by our own rules, under our own power, and celebrating our achievements—a futile endeavor that underscores the inherent incapacity of human effort to secure true recovery. It's a recognition that, in the realm of addiction, the destination called "recovery" remains elusive, replaced by a daily pilgrimage marked by faith and dependence on God.

This book is a lantern in the darkness, casting light on the theological underpinnings of addiction and recovery. Herein, the reader will confront the raw truth that the struggle against addiction is not merely a battle of willpower or a psychological chess match; it is spiritual warfare, a clash between the forces of hopelessness and the redemptive grace of a higher power.

The Impossible Prize invites readers into a profound dialogue with their vulnerabilities, urging them to relinquish the futile pursuit of self-made solutions and instead turn their gaze toward the divine.

Central to this exploration is the acknowledgment that addiction, like a relentless adversary, cannot be overcome through sheer human effort. It demands a God-given humility, recognizing our desperate need for a power greater than ourselves to lead us to sobriety and sanity. Through theological reflections, we navigate the complex terrain of surrender, repentance, and the transformative work of grace. In this context, theology becomes a compass guiding us through the intricacies of addiction, helping us discern the spiritual undercurrents that fuel our struggles.

Yet, this is not a journey marred solely by shadows; it's a testament to the unyielding hope embedded in faith. The reader will explore the profound implications of recognizing addiction not as a mark of moral failure but as a manifestation of the deadness inherent in the human condition. *The Impossible Prize* redefines the narrative, replacing the stigmatizing language of shame with the compassionate vocabulary of grace.

In the book, the reader will engage with biblical narratives that resonate with the struggles of addiction—from the prodigal son yearning for restoration to the bound man liberated by the compassionate touch of Christ. These stories are poignant mirrors reflecting the universal human experience of seeking an unattainable prize, only to find it freely given by a merciful God.

As we navigate these theological waters, *The Impossible Prize* also invites readers to confront the uncomfortable reality that addiction is not always conquered but endured. It challenges us to redefine victory, shifting the focus from the eradication of the struggle to the faithful perseverance within it. Through theological exploration, we unearth the profound truth that recovery is not a finish line; it's a continuous acknowledgment of dependence on God's sustaining grace.

The following chapters delve into the nuances of theology and addiction, unraveling the threads that bind the two in an intricate dance. We explore the transformative power of community, the sacramental nature of recovery, and the theology of surrender. *The Impossible Prize* is not a roadmap but a companion—a fellow traveler on the arduous path toward understanding, acceptance, and ultimately, embracing a divine grace that surpasses the limits of our human striving.

Introduction

No temptation has overtaken you that is not
common to man. God is faithful, and he will not
let you be tempted beyond your ability, but with
the temptation, he will also provide the way of
escape, that you may be able to endure it.

—1 Corinthians 10:13

Addiction is a complex issue that has plagued human-ity for centuries. Many people who have an addiction often struggle to break free from the grips of their addic-tion, and many turn to various forms of treatment to overcome it. However, addiction is not just a physical ailment but also a spiritual one, and as such, it requires a deep understanding of both the human condition and the divine will. In this book, we will explore how the teachings of sixteenth-century theologian Martin Luther can help us understand and explain addiction and how we can use his insights to find a new life and hope through recovery and sobriety today.

Luther's teachings offer a unique perspective on addiction that can help us grasp its spiritual dimensions. Luther's theology is grounded in his understanding of the human condition and the nature of sin, which he saw as a pervasive force that affects every aspect of human life. In this sense, addiction can be seen as an extension of this basic human condition, in which individuals turn to substances or behaviors as false gods to find temporary relief from the pain and suffering of life.

Luther's insights can also help us understand why addiction can be so difficult to overcome and how it can lead to a sense of powerlessness and despair. His teachings on the life-changing power of grace and the power of God's will can also provide hope for those struggling with addiction by reminding them that their salvation ultimately depends on God's grace in Jesus Christ rather than their efforts.

Furthermore, Luther's musings on what makes one a theologian of the cross can provide a framework for understanding the transformative power of suffering in faith, an essential part of addiction recovery. In addiction recovery, individuals must confront their pain and suffering head-on to overcome their addiction, and Luther's insights can help us understand how this process works. By embracing the cross, individuals find a new life and hope during their struggles and learn to see their addiction not as a curse but as an opportunity for strengthening their relationship with Jesus Christ and increasing their charitableness towards others.

Martin Luther's teachings on the nature of God, sin, and redemption offer valuable insights into addiction and recovery. They can help us better understand the spiritual dimensions of this complex and difficult struggle. So, in the following chapters, we will explore how Luther's teachings can help us recognize that addiction is more than simply a physical or mental affliction; it is a false god. Likewise, Luther's theology can help us fully appreciate the bondage of addiction, the importance of the theology of the cross in recovery, the dichotomy of faith and addiction, the importance of God's election of sinners through his word and the sacraments in recovery, and how Luther's teachings on vocation can help individuals in recovery find meaning and purpose in their lives. Thus, the book will proceed as follows:

Chapter 1: Luther's Definition of a False God and Addiction

To summarize Luther's explanation of the First Commandment in the Small Catechism, a god is whatever we fear, love, and trust more than anything else. In addiction, we can see how individuals turn to substances or behaviors as false gods, seeking solace, comfort, and escape from their troubles. They find temporary relief in their addiction, but it ultimately fails to provide lasting peace or happiness. Understanding addiction in this light can help us grasp the seriousness of the issue and begin to identify ways to address it.

Chapter 2: Luther's *Bondage of the Will* and Addiction

In his treatise on the *Bondage of the Will*, Luther argues that humans are powerless to save themselves from their sins and can only be saved by God's grace. A sense of powerlessness often characterizes addiction, and Luther's understanding of the human condition can help us better understand and explain why addiction can be so difficult to overcome. His emphasis on the role of grace and the power of God's will can also provide hope for those struggling with addiction.

Chapter 3: Luther's Theology of the Cross and Addiction Recovery

Luther's theology of the cross emphasizes the importance of suffering and how it can lead to renewed faith and a radical change in life. In addiction recovery, individuals must confront their pain and suffering head-on to overcome their addiction, and Luther's insights can help us understand how this process works. By embracing the cross, individuals find new life and hope amid their struggles and learn to see their addiction not as a curse but as an opportunity to enjoy a closer relationship with Jesus Christ and experience a new, sober life.

Chapter 4: Luther's Formulation of *Simul Iustus et Peccator* and Addiction

Luther's teaching on the Christian as *simul iustus et peccator* - simultaneously justified and sinful - helps us understand the dichotomy between faith and addiction. Addiction can make individuals feel as though they are irredeemable or unworthy of God's love, but Luther's insights remind us that even the most faithful believers are still sinners. This understanding can help those struggling with addiction recognize that they are not alone in their struggles and that God's grace in Jesus Christ is available to them no matter what.

Chapter 5: Luther's Teachings on Election and the Sacraments and Addiction

Luther's emphasis on God's election and the sacraments can provide hope for those struggling with addiction. Individuals receive God's grace and forgiveness through the Holy Spirit's preachers and the sacraments. Luther's teaching on election reminds us that God has chosen us despite our sinfulness, even when we consider ourselves the worst of all sinners. This can help individuals struggling with addiction to see in the cross of Christ that they are loved and chosen by God and can receive hope in their struggles.

It is the mission of this book to make clear that addicts are not doomed individuals in the hands of an angry God. Addicts are not doomed to die as hopeless cases. Addicts are the men and women for whom Jesus died on the cross to set free from sin, death, and the devil, which includes dying for their addiction and all the harm it's produced in their lives and the lives of others. An addict, like any sinner, is an individual to whom God sends a preacher to announce, "For Jesus' sake, you are forgiven. Be at peace."

Chapter 1

Luther's Definition of a False God and Addiction

What is addiction, really? It is a sign, a signal, a symptom of distress. It is a language that tells us about a plight that must be understood.

—Alice Miller, *Breaking Down the Wall of Silence: The Liberating Experience of Facing Painful Truth*

Part 1: What Is Addiction?

Addiction is defined as a chronic, relapsing disorder characterized by compulsive drug seeking and use despite the harmful consequences. It involves changes in the brain's reward, motivation, and memory circuits, which can lead to uncontrollable drug-seeking and drug-taking behavior.[1]

According to the American Psychiatric Association's *Diagnostic and Statistical Manual of Mental Disorders, Fifth Edition* (DSM-5), addiction is characterized by several key features, including an inability to control drug use, continued use despite

---

[1] National Institute on Drug Abuse, 2020.

negative consequences, and withdrawal symptoms when drug use is stopped.[2]

Additionally, addiction can lead to physical and psychological dependence on drugs or other substances, which can cause individuals to prioritize drug use over other aspects of their lives, such as work, school, or relationships.[3]

Overall, addiction is a complex and multifaceted disorder that can have severe consequences for individuals, families, and communities. Therefore, a comprehensive approach to treatment and prevention that addresses the biological, psychological, and social factors contributing to its development and maintenance is required.

Further, the basic text for Alcoholics Anonymous, called *Alcoholics Anonymous* (aka The Big Book), describes addiction to alcohol as a physical and mental compulsion to drink that results from an abnormal reaction to alcohol. That is, the individual cannot differentiate between normal drinking and excessive drinking. The Big Book notes, "Here is the fellow who has been puzzling you, especially his lack of control. He does absurd, incredible, tragic things while drinking. He is a real Dr. Jekyll and Mr. Hyde."[4]

But why? Why does the alcoholic behave like this? The Big Book goes on to explain that:

---

[2] American Psychiatric Association, 2013.

[3] World Health Organization, 2018.

[4] *Alcoholics Anonymous: The Story of How Many Thousands of Men and Women Have Recovered from Alcoholism*, Fourth Edition (New York City: Alcoholics Anonymous World Services, Inc., 2001), 21.

the truth, strange to say, is usually that he has no more idea why he took the first drink than you have. Some drinkers have excuses with which they are satisfied part of the time. But in their heart, they really do not know why they do it. Once this malady has a real hold, they are a baffled lot. There is the obsession that somehow, someday, they will beat the game. But they often suspect they are down for the count.[5]

The Big Book also describes addiction as a progressive illness that can lead to physical, mental, and spiritual deterioration. This is due in part to the fact that, over time, the individual's tolerance for alcohol increases, leading them to drink more and more to achieve the same effect. Such tolerance is a physical phenomenon where the body adapts to the presence of alcohol and requires increasingly larger amounts to produce the same effect. This can lead to a dangerous cycle of increased consumption and physical damage.

Overall, the Big Book of AA portrays addiction similarly to the previously mentioned descriptions, as a complex and multifaceted phenomenon that involves both physical and mental factors. Like the previous descriptions, the Big Book emphasizes the importance of abstinence as the only effective solution to addiction and provides a framework for individuals to achieve and maintain sobriety.

But what about the addict's soul? How does one recover what is seemingly lost and cannot be grasped by human hands? Do these standard, accepted definitions of addiction go deep enough to explain the roots of addiction?

---

[5] Ibid., 23.

Part 2: How Addiction Becomes Our God

What if we consider another approach to addiction that begins with a theological explanation? What if we start by admitting that our addiction goes deeper than physical and psychological dependence? What if we begin by confessing that the thing we are addicted to has become our god?

In the Bible, for example, we get a picture of how addiction can become a god. The apostle Paul, in his letter to the Christians in Rome, writes, "...they exchanged the truth about God for a lie and worshiped and served the creature rather than the Creator, who is blessed forever! Amen" (Rom 1:25). In this verse, the apostle is describing how people can become so focused on material possessions or physical pleasures that they begin to worship and serve them instead of the true God.

Another example is found in the story of the Israelites in the book of Exodus, where they turn away from God and begin to worship a golden calf they have made. This idol becomes the sole focus of their worship, and they are willing to sacrifice for it, even willingly disobeying God's command that they will "put no other gods before my face" (Ex 20:3, translation mine).

These examples demonstrate how, when we become addicted to something, we can easily prioritize it over the true God and willingly allow it to become our god. Addiction can then cause us to worship and serve something other than God, and this can ultimately lead us away from the truth about God, ourselves, and the nature of our addiction, resulting in habitual, self-sabotaging, self-destructive choices.

Adding to the previous biblical teachings, when we view addiction in light of Martin Luther's definition of a god – a god being something which we fear, love, and trust above all things – we begin with the jarring truth that we fear, love, and trust something more than the God who created and redeemed us.[6] Then we recognize that addiction not only involves a powerful attachment to a substance or behavior, which takes precedence over other priorities in a person's life; it drives us away from the source of our overall health and well-being.

Starting our examination of addiction in this way, we quickly become aware of the truth that addiction is more than just a physical or psychological affliction. It is a form of worship or devotion, as the individual's thoughts, actions, and emotions are taken captive to satisfy their craving or dependency.

In addiction, fear, love, and trust become centered on the substance or behavior that is the object of addiction. The individual may fear the consequences of not having access to their addiction, love the euphoric sensations or escape it provides, and trust that it will deliver relief from emotional pain or physical distress. Over time, the addictive substance or behavior becomes a source of security and comfort, and the individual becomes deeply entrenched in their attachment as they grow more and more dependent on a capricious, unforgiving god.

This dynamic of fear, love, and trust forms the subtext of every interaction between God and his people

---

[6] Martin Luther, "Luther's Small Catechism," in *The Book of Concord: The Confessions of the Evangelical Lutheran Church*, ed. Robert Kolb and Timothy J. Wengert (Minneapolis: Fortress Press, 2000), 351.

in the Bible. In the story of King Saul in 1 Samuel 15, God commands Saul to destroy the Amalekites, but Saul disobeys and spares their king and some of the best livestock. When the prophet Samuel confronts Saul about his disobedience, Saul responds by saying he fears the people and listens to their voices instead of obeying God's command. As a result of Saul's disobedience and fear of the people, God rejects him as king.

Likewise, in the account of the rich young ruler in Mark 10:17-27, a materially wealthy young man asks Jesus what he must do to inherit eternal life, and Jesus tells him to sell all he has and give it to the poor. However, the young man loves his possessions more than God, so he goes away sad and doesn't follow after Jesus.

And we are no different, even though more than two thousand years stand between us, the rich young man and Saul. In the present, the fear component of addiction can also be seen in the anxiety and distress that addicts experience when they are unable to engage in their addictive behavior. For example, a person addicted to alcohol may experience extreme anxiety and fear when they are unable to obtain their next drink. Similarly, a person addicted to gambling may feel intense fear and panic when they are unable to place a bet or engage in other gambling activities.

Similar to fear, the love component of addiction is evident in the way that addicts often prioritize their addictive behavior above all else. This can be seen in the way that addicts will frequently sacrifice their relationships, careers, and other important aspects of their lives to continue engaging in their addiction. A person addicted to drugs may prioritize their drug use over their job, their family, and their health, even if doing so leads to severe negative consequences.

Finally, trusting something more than the true God can be found in the story of the Israelites in Numbers 13-14. God promises to give the Israelites the land of Canaan, but when the spies return from their reconnaissance mission, ten of them provide a negative report, causing the people to fear the inhabitants of the land and doubt God's promise. As a result of their lack of trust, the Israelites are unable to enter the promised land until after they have wandered in the wilderness for forty years.

Trusting in a false god is just as evident in the way that addicts often rely on their addictive behavior to provide them with a sense of comfort or relief from their problems. This can be seen in the way that addicts will often turn to their addiction as a way to cope with stress, anxiety, or other negative emotions. A person addicted to food, for example, may turn to binge eating as a way to cope with stress or emotional pain, even if doing so leads to negative consequences such as weight gain, health problems, and social isolation.

And so, like any false deity that we turn to for help, addiction will demand immense sacrifices from those who worship it. The individual will neglect important responsibilities, relationships, and personal health to maintain their addiction. Even when the negative consequences of addiction become apparent, the individual will continue to prioritize their attachment over other aspects of their life. As the previous biblical examples demonstrate, there are serious repercussions when we fear, love, and trust something more than the true God. We miss out on blessings and fail to receive what God has promised us because we avoid seeking his guidance and following his will for our lives.

Therefore, with these three components of false belief and addiction in front of us, Martin Luther's definition of what a god is, which is to fear, love, and trust something more than the true God, is an apt description of addiction. Furthermore, as Luther writes in the Large Catechism, "A "god" is the term for that to which we are to look for all good and in which we are to find refuge in all need."[7]

In this light, addiction can be seen as a false god that addicts worship and rely on, even though doing so ultimately leads to severe, negative consequences and harms both the addict and those around them. Just as with any false god, addiction ultimately fails to deliver on its promises, leading the addict through euphoria and an escape from pain and struggle into insanity, incarceration, or self-annihilation. As a consequence, individuals with addiction will find that their addiction becomes increasingly costly, both in terms of the harm it causes to their own lives and the lives of those around them. As the addiction continues to demand more and more from them, addicts will experience deteriorating physical and mental health, strained relationships with loved ones, financial difficulties, legal problems, and, worst of all, a sense that God has cursed or abandoned them.

---

[7] Martin Luther, "Luther's Large Catechism," in *The Book of Concord: The Confessions of the Evangelical Lutheran Church*, ed. Robert Kolb and Timothy J. Wengert (Minneapolis: Fortress Press, 2000), 386.

This sense of abandonment can further lead individuals to act in kind, neglecting or even abandoning the things they truly value in life, such as their faith, relationships, work, and moral courage. Addiction becomes the primary focus of their life, eclipsing all other priorities and values, ultimately leading them astray and causing them to lose sight of what is truly important, which stems entirely from their false worship of an idol that demands they sacrifice everything, even their lives, to it.

Part 3: How We Worship Addiction

Worship is the act of ascribing worth to something or someone. It acknowledges that something or someone is worthy of our devotion and adoration. Whether or not we want to admit it, worship is fundamental to human nature, rooted in our desire to find meaning and purpose.

In the Bible, there are two types of worship: true and false. True worship is ascribing worth to God, the one true God, the almighty Father, worthy of all our devotion and adoration. False worship, on the other hand, is the act of ascribing worth to something or someone other than the one true God. This false worship is called idolatry, worshipping a false god, as it puts something or someone in the place of our Heavenly Father.

We see an example of this when the Israelites "did whatever is right in their hearts" during the times of the Judges. They turned from worshipping the Lord their God to genuflecting in reverence before the altars of

Baals and Ashteroth poles. This led them to engage in every spiritual and moral perversion imaginable.

But that's the trajectory of false worship. False worship leads to disregarding the things that should be prioritized in life, including one's relationship with God, familial responsibilities, and social obligations. It quickly deviates from the divine order of things, which disrupts the harmony and balance intended by God. And ultimately, it is a spiritual betrayal that hinders individuals from living out their calling to love and serve God and their fellow human beings.

This is depicted in Exodus 29:3-4, when Israel is forbidden from worshiping idols or other gods besides the one true God because false worship will lead Israel to disregard the things that should be prioritized in life, such as their God, their families, friends, and responsibilities. Likewise, Jesus says in Matthew 6:24 that no one may serve two masters. Either they will hate the one and love the other, or they will be devoted to the one and despise the other. As he says to Israel in the wilderness, Jesus again tells his first-century listeners that there is grave danger in trying to serve two masters, that is, two gods.

In the same way, the addict will eventually try to serve both their addiction and their desire for a healthy, fulfilling life, but ultimately, the addiction will win out, and the addict will be consumed by it. But this idol is very cunning and deceitful, so the object of worship for the addict can take many forms, such as drugs, alcohol, sex, gambling, or food. But, regardless of the form it takes, addiction is always a powerful force that has a devastating impact on the addict's life. Addiction will lead to spiritual, physical, psychological, and social problems as the addict becomes increasingly isolated and disconnected from the people and activities that once gave their life meaning and purpose.

So, this approach to understanding worship can provide a useful framework for understanding addiction and its impact on the addict's life. At its roots, addiction is a form of false worship, as the addict is worshipping a false god. The object of addiction takes the place of God in the addict's life, and the pursuit of pleasure or relief becomes the central focus of their life. This false worship then violates the command against false gods because the addict has put something or someone in the place of the true God.

On the other hand, true worship involves acknowledging that the true God is a God of grace and mercy. He is the source of all value and worth in life. Thus, to overcome addiction as a form of false worship, it is necessary to replace the false god of addiction with the true God who reveals himself to sinners on the cross of Jesus Christ. Afterward, he enriches them by leading them into meditation on his words in the Bible, prayer, and attending religious worship services to hear his preachers declare the good news of the Gospel of Jesus Christ, which unconditionally forgives sinners.

Again, we quickly see that the spiritual component of addiction recovery is essential for overcoming addiction as a form of false worship. It is only by replacing the false god of addiction with the true God who is revealed in Jesus Christ that the addict can find lasting freedom from their slavery to addiction.

The apostle Paul writes in Romans 6:16, "Do you not know that if you present yourselves to anyone as obedient slaves, you are slaves of the one whom you obey, either of sin, which leads to death, or of obedience, which leads to righteousness?" This verse warns us that when we obey something or someone other than the God who forgives sinners, we become enslaved to them. In addiction, the individual becomes a slave to their substance or behavior, unable to resist the urge to engage in it even when it is harmful to themselves and others.

With this in mind, we must admit that overcoming addiction is not easy. Addiction is a chronic physical, mental, and spiritual disease that requires ongoing support and management. Recovery, then, is a holistic process involving mind, body, and soul, and as difficult as it may be to accept when it occurs, relapse is a common part of that process. However, by understanding addiction as a form of false worship and addressing all of its components, beginning with the individual's relationship with God, it is possible to achieve lasting freedom from addiction. But there are still challenges, even after the addict receives freedom from addiction through faith in Jesus Christ and participation in a program of recovery.

One of the key challenges in addressing addiction as a form of false worship is restraining the stigma and shame that is often associated with addiction. Addicts are frequently seen as weak or immoral, and the shame associated with addiction can prevent addicts from seeking help. However, it is important to understand that addiction is a spiritual disease that results in harmful, immoral choices. Like any other disease, it requires treatment and support. Still, since, at its root, it is a spiritual affliction, it requires constantly hearing the forgiveness of sins preached in Jesus' name and being shown sympathy and compassion by others.

Another challenge in addressing addiction as a form of false worship is the lack of theological resources and person-to-person support available to addicts in so many churches. Addiction treatment can be expensive, and many addicts lack access to affordable treatment options. This is where congregational resources, such as pastoral care, support groups that focus on addiction's theological and social components, and sober environments grounded in grace and mercy, can be helpful.

This is all to say that addressing addiction as a form of false worship requires a shift in our theological and societal attitudes toward addiction. Instead of seeing addiction as unforgivable or as nothing more than a moral failure, we must recognize it as a spiritual disease that requires forgiveness and compassion and a physical and psychological disease that needs treatment and support. This is why we must recognize the spiritual component of addiction and the importance of replacing the false god of addiction with the true God revealed in Jesus Christ's life, death, and resurrection so that the whole person is addressed, receiving help for their body, mind, and soul.

Finally, to fully understand addiction as a form of false worship, it is also important to consider the role of the self in addiction. Whether we want to confront this truth or not, the self is at the center of worship. In true worship, the self is directed towards God and finds its true identity and purpose concerning God. However, in false worship, the self becomes the center of worship and seeks to find its identity and purpose in the false god.

This dynamic is abundantly apparent in addiction, where the addict becomes so consumed with the pursuit of pleasure or relief that their own identity and purpose become tied up in the object of addiction. They may begin to see themselves as a "drinker" or a "drug user" rather than as unique individuals, creatures of God gifted by him with strengths, weaknesses, and inherent value.

As the apostle John warned in 1 John 2:16, "For all that is in the world—the desires of the flesh and the desires of the eyes and pride of life—is not from the Father but is from the world." So, there is always a temptation for the addict to indulge in physical pleasures and desires, which leads to further harmful behavior. In addiction, the addict is driven by not only a physical desire for pleasure but relief from pain, leading them to engage in behaviors that are harmful to themselves and others.

So, overcoming addiction as a form of false worship requires a shift in the addict's understanding of themselves and their relationship to God and the world. This involves developing a sense of self-worth and purpose grounded in a relationship with Jesus Christ, specifically, the forgiveness of sins pronounced in his name and the mutual consolation and comfort of other believers. It also involves addressing the underlying psychological and social factors that contribute to the addict's sense of identity and purpose. This will also help the addict appreciate that false gods and false worship have deceived them, leading them to develop habits that locate their piety and devotion in what has been killing them and to shift their allegiances from what is false and deadly to what is true and vital.

Part 4: Our Piety and Devotion to Addiction

Piety is the quality of being devoted to something or someone, but ultimately, it involves living a life centered on God's will and guided by the teachings of God's published will in the Bible. On the other hand, devotion to God is giving oneself completely to him and living a life of service. Both piety and devotion stand on the belief that God is the most important aspect of life and that our ultimate goal is to live a life that is pleasing to him through faith in Jesus Christ.

However, addiction can be seen as a perversion of piety and devotion in that it involves a similar kind of all-encompassing devotion to a particular object or behavior. Addiction is a state of living where an individual becomes fixated on a specific substance or behavior to the extent that it takes over their life and becomes the primary focus of their thoughts and actions. Addiction also affects the brain and alters its chemistry, making it difficult for individuals to control their cravings and behavior or recognize that the object of their devotion is harming them.

While addiction can take many different forms, such as substance abuse, gambling, or internet addiction, the basic mechanism is the same: the brain's reward system is hijacked, and the individual becomes trapped in a cycle of compulsive behavior, seeking out the addictive substance or activity to experience a rush of pleasure and reward.

From a theological perspective, addiction can be seen as a false form of piety in which the addictive substance or behavior is worshipped in place of God. Instead of living a life that is centered on God's will, the individual's life is centered on the addiction, with all other concerns and responsibilities taking a back seat.

In this way, addiction can also be seen as a kind of false devotion, in which the individual is giving themselves over completely to the addiction rather than to God. Instead of living a life of service to the true God, the individual is serving their addiction, constantly seeking out the next fix or hit, and devoting all of their energy and resources to sustaining the addiction.

We see this kind of false piety in the Bible with the Pharisees. The Pharisees are a group of religious leaders known for their strict adherence to religious rules and rituals. Still, Jesus also criticized them for their hypocrisy and lack of true faith. In Matthew 23:25-28, Jesus condemns the Pharisees, saying,

> Woe to you, scribes and Pharisees, hypocrites! For you clean the outside of the cup and the plate, but inside they are full of greed and self-indulgence. You blind Pharisee! First clean the inside of the cup and the plate, that the outside also may be clean.

This passage can be applied to addiction, too, as addiction often involves a similar kind of outward appearance of success and control. At the same time, the inner life of the addict is characterized by fear, shame, and a lack of self-control. Addicts often strive to maintain their outward appearance by hiding their addiction from others, lying or making excuses to cover their behavior, or insisting that they are in control of their addiction, even when they are not.

Another example of false piety in the Bible following a similar trajectory is in Jesus' parable about the

Pharisee and the Tax Collector in Luke 18:9-14. Jesus tells a parable about a Pharisee who boasts about his piety and a tax collector who humbly asks for mercy. Jesus teaches that the tax collector is justified before God, not the self-righteous Pharisee.

This story reminds us that true devotion involves humility and a recognition of our selfish shortcomings. For those struggling with addiction, it can be easy to fall into a cycle of shame and self-condemnation, but Jesus teaches us that God's forgiveness and love are always available to us when we approach him like the tax collector, with humility and sincerity.

In both examples, the Bible teaches us that true piety and devotion require an inward change of the heart rather than just an outward appearance of religious observance or self-control. Similarly, recovery from addiction often requires a similar kind of inward transformation, where addicts must confront the root causes of their addiction and pray that God will change their hearts, transforming their inner lives to achieve lasting, holistic freedom and health.

This is vitally important, as has been noted. To repeat, one of the key aspects of addiction is the way that it can take over the individual's life to the point where all other concerns and responsibilities become secondary. This is because addiction alters the brain's reward system, making the addictive substance or behavior the primary focus of the individual's attention and motivation.

This is a form of idolatry in which the addictive substance or behavior is worshipped in place of God. Just as the Israelites were tempted to worship false idols instead of the true God, so too are addicts tempted to worship the addiction instead of living a life that is centered on their relationship with Jesus.

Moreover, addiction can be seen as a kind of false righteousness in which the individual believes that they are doing the right thing by indulging in the addiction. This false righteousness is similar to the legalism that Jesus rejects, in which individuals think that they can earn their way into heaven by following a strict set of rules and rituals.

In the case of addiction, the individual may believe that they are doing the right thing by satisfying their cravings and urges and that they are entitled to do so because of the pleasure and relief that it brings. This false righteousness can be a powerful barrier to recovery, as the individual may feel that they are doing the right thing and that others are wrong to try and stop them.

This then results in one becoming spiritually blind. The addict is unable to see the harm that their addiction is causing to their relationship with God, to themselves, and to those around them. This spiritual blindness is similar to the blindness that Jesus sees in the Pharisees, who are so caught up in their legalism that they are unable to see the true message of the Gospel, that he "comes to seek and save the lost" (Luke 19:10).

In the case of addiction, the individual becomes so fixated on their addiction that they are unable to see the damage that it is causing to their health, relationships, and overall well-being. They are in denial about the extent of their problem and resist any attempts to seek help or change their behavior.

This spiritual blindness can become a major obstacle to recovery, as the individual may not even realize that they have a problem or believe that they are in control of their addiction. It may take a major crisis, such as a health emergency or legal trouble, to finally break through this blindness and motivate the individual to seek help.

This is where the biblical teaching about grace is so critical. Grace is the unmerited favor that God extends to sinners. As the apostle Paul writes in Romans 5:6, "For while we were still weak, at the right time Christ died for the ungodly." Only through God's grace can we be saved, and no amount of piety or devotion to anything or anyone can help us earn our salvation.

This message of grace is, therefore, especially vital to those struggling with addiction, as many feel that they are unworthy of help or forgiveness because of the real-world consequences of their addiction. However, the message of God's grace in Jesus Christ teaches us that we are all sinners and that God's forgiveness and love are available to all people because Jesus died for the sins of the ungodly, which is all of us.

In the context of addiction, this means that even those who have struggled with addiction for years and who have caused harm to themselves and others can still receive hope and healing through the grace of God when they are pronounced forgiven in Jesus' name. It also means that those who are trying to help individuals struggling with addiction should approach them with compassion, recognizing that addiction is a complex and difficult condition that, most of all, begs for the kind of grace and mercy only Jesus can provide.

The addict, therefore, does not need to despair. They have simply been looking in the wrong places for help from those things that are not the true God. And the Bible teaches us that we need God's strength and grace to overcome difficult challenges, including addiction. For example, in Philippians 4:13, the apostle Paul writes, "I can do all things through him who strengthens me." This verse reminds us that we must not rely on our willpower alone to overcome addiction but on the strength and power of the God who was crucified for the sins of the world to help us in our struggles.

In addition, God will not turn away from the addict, as if he is too shocked by that individual's behavior to save them. Instead, as he did to the Samaritan woman at the well in John 4:1-42, Jesus will meet and engage us where we are and reveal that he knows everything about our past and current struggles. And despite what we or others think, Jesus offers us living water in baptism that transforms our lives through his forgiveness and love.

Jesus doesn't see the addict as an outcast or someone worthy of scorn. Instead, through the power of his grace, he changes the lives of addicts so that, in faith, they can see themselves as God sees them. And rather than being left alone by God to fight a losing battle with addiction, God sends a preacher to us in all our struggles, isolation, and defeats by addiction to announce that there is always hope where he is because of his forgiveness and love are available to everyone who hungers and thirsts for them.

So, addiction can take over an individual's life, leading to false piety, false devotion, and spiritual blindness. However, the message of grace and mercy declared in Jesus' name by his preachers gives hope and healing to all who seek it and will strengthen and encourage individuals to overcome addiction and reclaim a life lived in a relationship with a gracious and forgiving God rather than enslaved to an addiction that demands that they sacrifice their lives to it.

By recognizing the dangers of addiction and the power of grace, we can walk with addicts, treating them the same way the father welcomes the prodigal son home in Luke 15:11-32. In the parable, a young man asks his father for his inheritance and then squanders it on wild living. When he finds himself destitute and hungry, he returns to his father, who welcomes him back with open arms. The older brother, however, is resentful of his younger brother's behavior and refuses to join in the celebration. This story highlights the dangers of self-indulgence and the importance of forgiveness. For those struggling with addiction, the story can also serve as a reminder that it is never too late to turn things around and seek help.

In the same way, we can declare to addicts that with the true God, who is the Christ who died for the sins of the world, they do not have to be held captive by their addictions. Jesus has come to set them free through his grace and forgiveness to live a life centered on God's will and guided by his teachings, especially those that focus on Jesus Christ crucified for the sin of the world and the forgiveness and new life that it delivers.

Chapter 2

Luther's *Bondage of the Will* and Addiction

We see that substance addictions are only
one specific form of blind attachment to
harmful ways of being, yet we condemn the
addict's stubborn refusal to give up something
deleterious to his life or to the life of others.
Why do we despise, ostracize and punish the
drug addict, when as a social collective, we share
the same blindness and engage in the same
rationalizations?

—Gabor Maté, *In the Realm of
Hungry Ghosts: Close Encounters
with Addiction*

Addiction has been a subject of much discussion and
debate over the years. Many different theories have been
proposed to explain why people become addicted to
substances or behaviors, but what if we turn instead to
a five-hundred-year-old debate about the role of the
human will in salvation? As far-fetched as it may seem,
Martin Luther's debate with Erasmus of Rotterdam in
1525 on what role the human will plays in a person's

salvation has a great deal to teach us about addiction and recovery today.

Erasmus' treatise on *The Freedom of the Will* proposes that the human will plays some role in salvation. Luther contrarily asserts that humans cannot choose to follow God on their own and must rely on divine intervention to guide them. So then, what does this have to do with addiction and recovery?

The Bondage of the Will, as Luther titled it, is a powerful exploration of the nature of human will and how it is captivated by either sin or grace. While it may seem at first glance that this work has little to do with addiction, a closer examination reveals that Luther's insights can be incredibly valuable for understanding the complex and destructive dynamic of being captivated by addiction.

Part 1: The Nature of the Will and the Bondage of Sin

In *The Bondage of the Will*, Luther argues that human will is not truly free but rather is bound by sin and the influence of Satan. He asserts that "if God is in us, Satan is out of us, then it is present with us to will only good. But if God is not in us, Satan is, and then it is present with us to will only evil."[1] According to Luther, the will is not a neutral faculty that can choose between good and evil; rather, it is enslaved to sin and can only choose what is opposed to God's will.

---

[1] Martin Luther, *The Bondage of the Will*, trans. J.I. Packer and O.R. Johnston (Grand Rapids: Fleming H. Revell, 1957), 147.

He writes, "the man's will is like a beast standing between two riders. If God rides, it wills and goes where God wills. . . . If Satan rides, it wills and goes where Satan wills."[2] This biblical teaching, from Psalm 73:22, of the will as a "beast" that can be ridden by either God or Satan is a powerful depiction of how our choices and actions are shaped by larger spiritual forces. It asserts that we are not autonomous agents, making rational decisions based on our desires and preferences, but rather that we are deeply influenced by external factors that we may not even be aware of.

Our only hope for salvation then lies in receiving the grace of God, which he freely bestows upon us through the death and resurrection of Jesus Christ. The "backspin," so to speak, of this confession is that the human will isn't free to choose God and salvation and has no power to do what God wills. Instead, since the fall of Adam and Eve, we have been slaves to sin and can only do good when we are helped by God's grace.

This captivation of the human will is a consequence of humanity's fall into sin. By the fall of Adam and Eve, free will has been lost, and all people have become the slaves of sin. Human beings are, therefore, not able to choose to follow God's will because they are fundamentally sinful and enslaved to their desires.

More than that, any attempt to free ourselves from the bondage of sin through our own choices or good works is futile. After the fall of Adam and Eve, our choices have no power to do anything but sin and to resist God's grace until we are taken captive by God's grace, as revealed in Jesus Christ. It is only through

---

[2] Ibid., 103.

God's grace, freely given through Jesus Christ's work for sinners, that the will can be transformed and freed from its captivation to sin.

In other words, Luther believes that humans can make choices, but these choices are ultimately determined by God, and we are unable to choose good without the help of divine intervention. This position is central to Luther's understanding of the human condition and has important implications for our understanding of addiction.

The fact that the human will is a captive to sin has significant implications for addiction. If we acknowledge that our will is not truly free but is instead shaped and directed by larger spiritual forces, then it follows that addiction can be seen as a manifestation of this bondage. Addicts are not simply making poor choices based on their prejudices and desires but rather are being driven by a powerful external force that they cannot control. In other words, addiction is not a simple matter of willpower but rather a powerful, debilitating spiritual phenomenon that requires deeper understanding and care than has yet been afforded to addicts.

As a consequence, to overcome addiction, individuals must first recognize that they are bound by forces beyond their control. This recognition can be difficult, as addicts often feel ashamed and guilt-ridden about their behavior and may be resistant to seeking help. However, by admitting the limitations of their own will and seeking help from God, individuals in recovery can begin to address the root causes of their addiction, trusting that God is at work overcoming addiction's grip on their lives.

Luther's insights into the limitations of humans underscore the importance of treating addiction as a whole-person phenomenon. Addiction is not simply a matter of behavior but is rooted in deep-seated spiritual afflictions that must be addressed to achieve lasting recovery. By addressing the underlying causes of addictive behavior, individuals in recovery gain greater awareness of their condition, build healthy coping mechanisms, and experience greater freedom and wholeness in their lives, trusting that, as the psalmist writes in Psalm 46:1, "God is our refuge and strength, a very present help in trouble."

From this perspective, Luther's argument with Erasmus about the nature of the will and the bondage of sin does have significant implications for addiction and recovery. The human will is not free but is enslaved to sin, which means that individuals struggling with addiction are not in control of their own choices and actions. Instead, their addiction has taken over, and they are powerless to resist its pull.

This deeper understanding of the human will and its bondage of sin is both humbling and liberating for individuals in recovery. On the one hand, it's humbling to realize that one's addiction is not a matter of weak willpower or personal failure but rather a symptom of a deeper spiritual condition. On the other hand, it is liberating to know that one's recovery does not depend solely on one's efforts and failures but is ultimately a gift of God's grace.

In practical terms, Luther's understanding of the will and its captivation to sin can inform the approach to addiction treatment and recovery. Rather than relying solely on individual effort, recovery can be seen as the action of God's forgiveness and grace in the individual's life that sets them free through the forgiveness of sins to seek pastoral guidance and support and a community of faith. This can and should also include participation in a supportive recovery community now that it's been revealed to them that they can rely on the power of God's promises to deliver forgiveness, new life, and the hope of eternal salvation no matter what condition they're in at the moment.

Overall, Luther's understanding of the nature of the will and the bondage of sin highlights the need for a holistic approach to addiction treatment and recovery, one that acknowledges the spiritual dimensions of addiction and recognizes the role of God's grace in the recovery process.

Part 2: Addiction as a Manifestation of Bondage

When we view addiction through the lens of Luther's assertions in his treatise, *The Bondage of the Will*, we can see how addiction distorts and perverts the individual's will. Addiction is not simply a matter of choosing to engage in destructive behaviors. Instead, it is a complex and often overwhelming dynamic of spiritual, physical, and psychological dependence that can be incredibly difficult, if not impossible, to break.

In light of Luther's view of the impotence of the human will, it is possible to see addiction as a manifestation of the human inability to control one's actions. Addiction can be seen as a sort of slavery in which the individual is held captive by their desires and impulses, unable to break free without divine intervention. Addicts may know intellectually that their behavior is destructive, but they are unable to overcome the powerful physical, psychological, and spiritual yearnings that drive them to continue using.

A striking example of this captivation of the will is found in the book of Exodus when the Israelites are enslaved in Egypt. Despite their suffering and cries for freedom, they are unable to free themselves from the oppression of their Egyptian taskmasters. In Exodus 6:9, the Israelites are described as being "too discouraged to believe" that God would rescue them.

Then, in Exodus 7-12, God sends a series of plagues to Egypt, culminating in the death of the firstborn, to compel Pharaoh to let the Israelites go. But, even after witnessing these miraculous signs and wonders, Pharaoh stubbornly refuses to release the Israelites until he is finally forced to do so by God's intervention.

This account demonstrates the reality of the bondage of the will, as the Israelites and even Pharaoh are unable to act contrary to their inclinations and desires without divine intervention. It is only through God's sovereign power and grace that the Israelites are ultimately freed from their bondage in Egypt, and even then, they still complain and rebel against God in the wilderness!

The cycle of addiction, too, can be seen as a manifestation of how sin distorts and perverts the will. And like Pharaoh and Israel, rather than seeking God's will and the good of others, addicts become consumed by their yearnings and cravings. They may engage in destructive behaviors that harm themselves and those around them and are unable to break free from their terminal course without divine intervention and grace.

Thus, if Luther were to write on the topic of the bondage of the will and addiction today, it's probable that he would assert that addiction is a form of spiritual compulsion and that it arises from the fact that the human will is enslaved to sinful desires and that addiction is not something that can be overcome through sheer willpower, but rather it requires a fundamental transformation of the will that can only be brought about by the grace of God delivered through a preacher declaring the forgiveness of sins in Jesus' name.

One of the most famous passages on this topic is from Romans 7:15-20, in which the apostle Paul writes:

> For I do not understand my own actions. For I do not do what I want, but I do the very thing I hate. Now if I do what I do not want, I agree with the law, that it is good. So now it is no longer I who do it, but sin that dwells within me. For I know that nothing good dwells in me, that is, in my flesh. For I have the desire to do what is right, but not the ability to carry it out. For I do not do the good I want, but the evil I do not want is what I keep on doing. Now if I do what I do not want, it is no longer I who do it, but sin that dwells within me.

This passage captures the sense of frustration and powerlessness that is often felt by those struggling with addiction. Paul's description of wanting to do good but being unable to carry it out resonates with the experience of a multitude of addicts who feel trapped by their addiction, unable to break free despite their best efforts.

In another passage, James 1:14-15, the author describes the process by which addiction takes hold:

> But each person is tempted when he is lured and enticed by his own desire. Then desire when it has conceived gives birth to sin, and sin when it is fully grown brings forth death.

This passage highlights the insidious nature of addiction, in which a desire germinates and grows, tempting one to fixate on something that is not the true God, something that then eventually leads to death. And that's the reality of addiction; it's a kind of spiritual death that reverberates throughout the Bible, and it is a theme that is particularly relevant to Luther's treatise on *The Bondage of the Will.*

Only through the grace of God in Jesus Christ can we expect to be set free from our bondage to sin because addiction is not merely a physical or psychological condition. It is a spiritual condition that involves the bondage of the will to sin and the insidious work of the devil to ride us away from the source of our life and salvation. As a consequence of this recognition that addiction is not merely a personal weakness or failure, but rather it is a spiritual battle that we cannot hope to win, it requires the intervention of God's grace to overcome.

So, the solution to addiction is then not simply to exert greater willpower or to try harder to quit. Instead, it involves God taking our will captive to himself through the forgiveness and grace delivered in Jesus' name by his preachers and the subsequent faith created as our life is transformed by the Holy Spirit, taking the reins away from Satan.

In summary, Luther's understanding of addiction as a manifestation of bondage holds that addiction is a spiritual condition that arises from the bondage of the will to sin, the world, and the devil. This tack emphasizes that addiction is not simply a personal failing, but rather, it is a spiritual battle that requires the intervention of God's grace to overcome. So, Luther's insights have important implications for how we understand and approach the problem of addiction, emphasizing the need for a spiritual transformation of the will rather than simply relying on personal willpower or other forms of self-help.

Part 3: Breaking the Cycle of Addiction Through Grace

While addiction can be a powerful manifestation of the bondage of the will, Luther's theology also offers hope for those struggling with addiction because central to Luther's message is the biblical teaching about God's grace, the unmerited love and favor of God that is freely given to all who believe in Jesus Christ through the forgiveness of their sins.

Luther's solution to the affliction of human bondage to sin emphasizes the importance of divine forgiveness and grace. Salvation is a gift of grace that is freely given by God and cannot be earned or achieved by human effort. Thus, Luther writes,

> Paul says this of the Gentiles - that it is given to them to hear and know Christ when previously they could not even think on Him, much less seek Him or prepare

themselves for Him by the power of 'free will.' From this instance, it is clear enough that grace comes so freely that no thought of it, and certainly no endeavor or desire after it, precedes its coming.[3]

Grace, then, is a powerful declaration that can break the cycle of addiction by transforming the will and redirecting it toward God's purposes. For addicts, this message of grace is, therefore, particularly powerful. It gives addicts hope that they can break free from the cycle of addiction, not through their efforts or willpower, but through the transformative power of God's love.

When an addict receives God's forgiveness and grace in faith as a gift, they are liberated from the powerful cravings and dependencies that have held them captive because God's grace is not given to righteous people but to sinners. It is not given to those who think they deserve it but to those who confess they don't deserve it. In other words, God's grace is only for those who have been taken captive by sin and the devil.

Likewise, throughout the Bible, there are numerous examples of individuals who struggle with the captivation of their will in various forms and are liberated by God's grace. One such example is the story of what happened to the Israelites after God liberated them from their slavery to Pharaoh. The Israelites had been enslaved in Egypt for generations, and when they were finally freed, they faced a long and difficult journey through the wilderness to reach the Promised Land, a land God promises is "flowing with milk and honey" (Ex 3:8).

---

[3] Ibid., 301.

During this journey, the Israelites struggle with addiction to food, complaining, and idolatry. They grumble about the lack of food and water, and when God provides for them in miraculous ways, they still long for the disgusting food they had been forced to eat in Egypt. They also build a golden calf as an idol to worship, even though God has delivered them from the oppression of Egypt's gods.

This account highlights the human condition of bondage to sin and the many forms that addiction can take. It also illustrates the destructive nature of addiction and how it can lead individuals and groups down a path of darkness and despair. However, the account of Israel in the wilderness also demonstrates that there is hope for redemption and healing through God's grace and mercy, even in the face of bondage that causes people to rebel against God's goodwill.

It is also important to note that the process of breaking the cycle of addiction is not straightforward. Addiction is a complex and multifaceted problem that requires a comprehensive approach to treatment and recovery. While the pronouncement of forgiveness and the message of God's grace is an essential component of this process, it must be coupled with practical strategies and resources that can help addicts break free from addiction's affliction in their daily lives.

Breaking the power of addiction's grip involves a combination of professional help, support from loved ones, and pastoral guidance. However, at the heart of this process is the recognition that true healing and freedom can only come through the power of divine grace delivered through the forgiveness of sins pronounced in Jesus' name.

In the context of addiction, preaching grace as God's unmerited favor brings about transformation and restoration in the individual's life. It is the power of God that strengthens individuals to break free from the power of addiction and find new life in Christ Jesus.

Thus, the first step in breaking the cycle of addiction through grace is to acknowledge the reality of the addiction and admit the need for help. This may involve seeking a pastor, professional treatment, joining a support group, or turning to a trusted friend or family member for support.

The second step is to pray for God to give the individual the strength to surrender their illusory control over their life and choices and trust in the power of God's grace to effect change in their life. This involves acknowledging that human efforts alone are not sufficient to overcome addiction and that true healing and freedom can only come through the power of God, who acts for us by sending the Holy Spirit with his preachers to declare that on account of Jesus Christ's work for us, forgiveness, new life, and eternal salvation is given *gratis*. In the context of addiction, this means recognizing that it is not our efforts that will break the bondage of addiction but rather the power of the Holy Spirit and God's Word working in us to bring about transformation and healing.

The third step is cultivating a relationship with God through meditating on and studying his published will in the Bible. This involves relying not on ourselves but praying and trusting that God will work in us to bring about lasting change.

The fourth step is to develop healthy habits and practices that support our recovery. This involves, for example, finding a pastor who preaches forgiveness and grace, joining a church of like-minded Christians who also need the liberating power of the Gospel to free them from their bondage to sin, making changes to our daily routine, setting boundaries around certain behaviors or activities, and seeking out supportive relationships and communities.

Part 4: Further Application of Luther's Theology to Addiction Treatment

As we have now seen, Luther's theological position about the captivation of the human will by sin and the devil and the role of grace and forgiveness in salvation has significant implications for addiction treatment. Even though addiction has deep roots in a person's psyche and environment, traditional treatment methods can often fall short of achieving lasting results because they do not acknowledge or consider the power of God's grace that transforms our will and affects true liberation from addiction. Thus, applying Luther's theological insights can provide a fresh perspective and offer hope to those struggling with addiction.

Since Luther's teachings emphasize the centrality of grace in the Christian life, this means that human beings are completely incapable of choosing God on their own due to Adam and Eve's fall into sin in the Garden of Eden. Luther's perspective also challenges the notion that a person can overcome addiction through sheer willpower or self-discipline. Rather, Luther believes that true change comes from the work of the Holy Spirit, who changes the heart and mind of the believer.

Luther professes a biblical revelation about the human will and salvation. The Bible constantly emphasizes the role of grace in overcoming sin. Ephesians 2:8-9 states, "For by grace you have been saved through faith. And this is not your own doing; it is the gift of God, not a result of works, so that no one may boast." This verse underscores the idea that salvation is a gift that cannot be earned but is freely given by God. In the context of addiction treatment, this means that individuals struggling with addiction can turn to God and rely on his grace to break them free from the bondage of addiction.

So, to repeat what was noted earlier in this chapter, in Romans 7:18-19, the apostle Paul writes a provocative statement about the human condition,

> For I know that nothing good dwells in me, that is, in my flesh. For I have the desire to do what is right, but not the ability to carry it out. For I do not do the good I want, but the evil I do not want is what I keep on doing. flesh. For I have the desire to do what is right, but not the ability to carry it out. For I do not do the good I want, but the evil I do not want is what I keep on doing.

This passage powerfully highlights the struggle that many individuals face when trying to overcome addiction. The desire to do what is right is present, but the ability to carry it out is lacking.

In the context of addiction treatment, this means that individuals struggling with addiction need to recognize that their addiction is not solely their fault and that they should not feel shame or guilt for their struggles. Instead, they are directed to turn to Jesus, the Lamb of God crucified for the sins of the world, and to rely on his grace and forgiveness, which possesses the power to overcome their addiction.

This focus on Jesus and not themselves reorients individuals to embrace their struggles and receive them in joy because, as the apostle Paul writes to the Christians in Colossae, "Now I rejoice in my sufferings for your sake, and in my flesh I am filling up what is lacking in Christ's afflictions for the sake of his body, that is, the church…" (Col 1:24). It also challenges the notion that success and prosperity are the ultimate goals of life, and instead encourages individuals to focus on their relationship with Jesus and their spiritual well-being. It reminds individuals that God is present with them in their struggles and working in their lives, even during difficult circumstances.

But this isn't a new approach. The Bible emphasizes the inevitability of suffering and trials in the life of every believer. James 1:2-4 states, "Count it all joy, my brothers, when you meet trials of various kinds, for you know that the testing of your faith produces steadfastness. And let steadfastness have its full effect, that you may be perfect and complete, lacking in nothing." Like Paul's encouragement to the Christians at Colossae, this passage highlights the reality that trials and difficulties often lead us to greater awareness of our dependence on a gracious God, which is a joy in itself as it reveals a deepening of our relationship with him.

In the context of addiction treatment, this means that individuals struggling with addiction should not view their struggles as a sign of failure but rather as an opportunity to pray and wait for God to work, strengthening them to resist the temptation to relapse and continue in sober living. They also trust that God is present with them in their struggles and that he is working in and through their difficulties to shape them into the people he wants them to be.

And so, applying Luther's theological insights about the human will and its bondage to sin and the devil to addiction treatment, we receive a fresh perspective and hope for individuals struggling with addiction. His emphasis on the centrality of grace and the transformative power of the Holy Spirit challenges the notion that addiction can be overcome through human effort alone. His perspective also highlights the importance of recognizing that addiction is not solely a personal choice or moral failing but rather a result of a fallen world that needs redemption.

Luther's insights remind us that God is present with us in our afflictions and struggles and is working in our lives, even and especially amid difficult circumstances. By embracing these insights, individuals struggling with addiction can find hope, healing, and transformed lives through the power of God's grace and mercy delivered through the forgiveness of sin declared in Jesus' name.

Chapter 3

Luther's Theology of the Cross and Addiction Recovery

> He who does not know Christ does not know
> God hidden in suffering… God can be found
> only in suffering and the cross.
>
> —Martin Luther, *Heidelberg
> Disputation,* Thesis 21

Luther's theology of the cross is a central tenet of his theological thinking that informs his understanding of the human condition, the nature of sin, and the means of redemption. As such, his theological perspective provides a useful approach to addiction recovery as a framework for understanding the nature of addiction, its effects on the individual and society, and the means of recovery.

The theology of the cross emerged out of Luther's spiritual struggles as he sought to understand the relationship between God and human beings. In contrast to the prevailing theological perspective of his time, which emphasized human efforts and good works as the means of salvation, Luther saw the cross of Christ as the ultimate expression of God's grace and love for humanity. For Luther, the cross is not simply an event in history but an ongoing reality that shapes the lives of believers and non-believers alike since "the love of God which lives in man loves sinners, evil persons, fools, and weaklings to make them righteous, good, wise, and strong."[1]

Luther's theology of the cross highlights the paradoxical nature of the Christian faith, in which weakness is strength, death is life, and suffering is glory. On the cross, Luther saw the ultimate expression of God's love, as Christ willingly took on the sins of humanity and suffered the consequences of our sins on behalf of all. This understanding of the cross challenges the prevailing cultural values of strength, power, and success and calls for a radical reorientation of our understanding of the human condition.

Luther's perspective is particularly relevant to addiction recovery, which involves confronting the negative consequences of one's actions and recognizing one's powerlessness over addiction. Luther's theology of the cross offers a powerful framework for understanding the paradoxical nature of addiction recovery, in which boldness and humility are essential components of true healing and sober life.

However, addiction is an extreme manifestation of the human will's captivity to sin, which is characterized by a self-centered and self-destructive orientation toward the world. Luther asserted that this orientation is a fundamental aspect of the human condition that,

---

[1] Martin Luther, "The Heidelberg Disputation," in *Luther's Works*, vol. 31: Career of the Reformer, ed. Harold J. Grimm (Saint Louis: Concordia Publishing House, 1957), 57.

therefore, requires radical intervention if any significant change is to occur, which can only be accomplished through the grace of God. As Luther writes, "the will outside of grace or in falling is unable not to fall and not to will evil by its own power. It is able, by the grace of God, not to fall or to stop falling."[2]

In addiction recovery, this reorientation is often facilitated through an act of surrender, in which individuals are compelled by God to acknowledge their powerlessness over their addiction and turn to him for help. This act of surrender is not simply a matter of giving up control but of being embraced by a gracious, loving God, and thus being embraced by a new way of living that is grounded in a bold confession of our sin, humility towards God, and service and self-giving love towards others.

Therefore, the theology of the cross offers a powerful vision of what this new way of living might look like, as it challenges us to embrace the paradoxical nature of the Christian faith, in which weakness is strength, death is life, and suffering is glory. In addiction recovery, this means embracing the reality that we are in bondage to sin and cannot free ourselves, that we need help, and that only God can fully heal and renew our lives.

Luther's theology of the cross also offers a powerful critique of the prevailing cultural values that often contribute to addiction and its negative consequences. The emphasis on strength, power, and success in contemporary culture can lead individuals to believe they can control their own lives and achieve their goals through

---

[2] Ibid., 59.

their efforts. This attitude can be particularly dangerous in the context of addiction. It can lead individuals to deny the reality of their addiction and the need for help, "because men do not know the cross and hate it, they necessarily love the opposite, namely, wisdom, glory, power, and so on."[3]

Focusing on success and achievement in contemporary culture can also create a competitive and individualistic environment that often leaves individuals feeling disconnected, isolated, and hopeless. This sense of disconnection and isolation can be particularly dangerous in the context of addiction, as it can lead individuals to turn to drugs and alcohol as a means of escape.

The theology of the cross challenges this perspective by refocusing our attention on the cross of Christ for our life and hope. Luther saw the ultimate expression of God's love for humanity in the cross. He writes, "This is the love of the cross, born of the cross, which turns in the direction where it does not find good which it may enjoy, but where it may confer good upon the bad and needy person."[4]

This perspective calls individuals to embrace a new way of living that is grounded in faith in Christ Jesus, engaging with a community of believers, connecting with others in relationships grounded in selflessness and charity, and finding solidarity with other addicts in recovery, seeking to address the societal factors that also contribute to an individual's addiction.

---

[3] Ibid., 54.
[4] Ibid., 57.

Part 1: What is the Theology of the Cross?

Luther's theology of the cross is based on his understanding of the cross of Christ. According to Luther, the cross is the ultimate symbol of God's grace and love. It is through the cross that God demonstrates his love for humanity, and it is through the cross that humanity is reconciled to God by Jesus' bloody suffering and death for the sins of the world.

However, Luther's understanding of the cross is not limited to a historical event. Instead, Luther believes that the cross is a continuing reality in the lives of believers. In other words, the cross is not just an event that happened in the past, but it is also a present reality that shapes the lives of Christians today when God sends his preachers to declare the good news to sinners that they are forgiven in Jesus' name.

One of the key ideas in Luther's theology of the cross, then, is the hiddenness of God. Luther believes that God is hidden in the suffering and weakness of the cross. This is in contrast to the traditional understanding of God as a powerful and triumphant figure. According to Luther, the true nature of God is revealed in the cross, which appears weak and foolish to the world, but to God, it is the revelation of his victory over sin, the world, and the devil. This perspective is based on the apostle Paul's assertion in 1 Corinthians 1:21 that "For since in the wisdom of God, the world did not know God through wisdom, it pleased God through the folly of what we preach to save those who believe." Thus, as Luther writes, "It is not sufficient for anyone and does him no good to recognize God in his glory and majesty unless he recognizes him in the humility and shame of the cross."[5]

Based on his reading of the Bible, Luther believes that God is present in the world, not in power and glory, but in suffering, poverty, and weakness. He argues that the cross is the ultimate symbol of God's presence and love for humanity. In other words, God is most clearly revealed in human suffering, weakness, and vulnerability.

In contrast to the theology of the cross, Luther also critiques what he calls the theology of glory. The theology of glory is the belief that God's glory can be found in human achievements and accomplishments. According to Luther, this idea is misguided because it focuses on human works rather than God's grace. Luther writes about the theology of glory in his Heidelberg Disputation: "A theologian of glory calls evil good and good evil. A theologian of the cross calls the thing what it actually is."[6] The theology of glory is thus a distorted understanding of reality because it calls evil good and good evil, whereas the theology of the cross sees things as they are. That is, the theology of the cross sees all things, especially the wisdom and works of God, through suffering and the cross of Jesus Christ.

The theology of glory accentuates the importance of understanding God's nature through his power, glory, and success. According to this theology, God's nature is revealed most clearly in his ability to do great things, to triumph over his enemies, and to bring success

---

[5] Ibid., 52.
[6] Ibid., 40.

to his people. Luther believes that people who adhere to the theology of glory are not concerned about their relationship with Jesus but are always using God as an excuse to look for ways to prove their righteousness and their ability to succeed in life.

This is why the theology of glory can be so harmful to individuals in recovery. It can lead them to believe that their success in overcoming addiction is solely dependent on their strength and willpower. This can create an unrealistic expectation of success and lead to disappointment and discouragement if they are unable to overcome their addiction on their own. It can also create a sense of pride and self-righteousness if they do succeed, which can be damaging to their relationships and their recovery.

However, Luther did not invent the theology of the cross and the theology of glory to serve as useful categories for academic debate. Instead, these two competing theologies are deeply rooted in the biblical narrative (in Jesus' crucifixion and resurrection, for example). In his first letter to the Christians at Corinth, the apostle Paul writes, "the word of the cross is folly to those who are perishing, but to us who are being saved it is the power of God" (1 Cor 1:18).

Paul argues that the cross is not a symbol of weakness, even though it appears that way to those looking for God in their achievements and accomplishments, but rather a symbol of God's power and love revealed in the humiliation, suffering, and death of Jesus. Jesus, who was crucified in our place and suffered the most humiliating and excruciating death that we deserved, is the ultimate embodiment of God's love for humanity.

This theme is repeated throughout the New Testament, particularly in the book of Hebrews. The author of Hebrews writes that Jesus "endured the cross, despising the shame, and is seated at the right hand of the throne of God" (Heb 12:2). The author argues that Jesus' sacrifice on the cross was not a sign of weakness or defeat, but rather a demonstration of God's love and power.

Furthermore, the theology of the cross is also evident in the story of the Israelites in the Old Testament. The Israelites are a people who are repeatedly oppressed, enslaved, and exiled. They face immense suffering and hardship, but God is faithful to his people and leads them through all their afflictions. Similarly, the book of Psalms is filled with laments and expressions of grief and suffering, but it also contains expressions of hope and trust in God's faithfulness.

One particularly relevant account is the story of Joseph in the book of Genesis. Joseph is sold into slavery by his brothers and faces years of hardship and imprisonment. But even in his suffering, God remains faithful to Joseph. It is through his suffering that God can use Joseph to save the Israelites from famine and oppression. As Joseph says to his brothers, who beg him not to punish them for the evil they had done to him, "As for you, you meant evil against me, but God meant it for good, to bring it about that many people should be kept alive, as they are today" (Gen 50:20). Joseph's story is a stark example of how God can use suffering and weakness for good and how even in hardship, God is present and at work.

On the other hand, the theology of glory is often associated with the story of the Tower of Babel in

Genesis 11. The people of Babel want to build a tower that will reach the heavens, and in doing so, they hope to make a name for themselves. But God sees their pride and arrogance and scatters them across the earth. Contrary to Joseph's story in Genesis 50, this account is often interpreted as a warning against the dangers of human pride and the desire for success and glory.

Understanding the theology of the cross can be extremely beneficial for individuals in recovery from addiction. Addiction is a form of suffering that can be extremely difficult to overcome. It can leave individuals feeling weak, vulnerable, and powerless. The theology of the cross offers a way of understanding God's response to this kind of suffering. It focuses us on God's presence amid human suffering, weakness, and vulnerability and that he is with individuals as they struggle to overcome their addiction, offering them hope and strength through faith in the grace of Christ.

For an addict in recovery, therefore, distinguishing between the theology of the cross and the theology of glory can be crucial for their spiritual and emotional well-being. A theology of the cross emphasizes the suffering and humility of Christ on the cross, which is a powerful message for addicts who are often experiencing their form of suffering and powerlessness. The theology of the cross teaches that true redemption comes through receiving the grace of Jesus Christ through the forgiveness of sins that were won for us through his suffering and death.

Opposed to this is a theology of glory that emphasizes the pursuit of personal achievement and success, which can be dangerous for addicts who tend to seek fulfillment through substances or other harmful behaviors. Understanding and embracing a theology of the cross can help an addict let go of their need for control and find comfort in the belief that their suffering has a greater purpose.

Moreover, distinguishing between these two theologies can help an addict avoid potential spiritual pitfalls in recovery. A theology of glory can lead to a focus on external measures of success and can be a breeding ground for pride and self-righteousness. But, a theology of the cross can cultivate humility, which is an essential component of recovery. Embracing the cross can help an addict recognize their limitations and turn to Jesus Christ for help and support. This can be an important shift in perspective for an addict who may have previously relied on their willpower or self-reliance, ultimately leading to relapse. By embracing a theology of the cross, an addict can find peace in their vulnerability and rely on God's grace to forgive them, create a new life for them, and give them hope that, as Jesus promises the man crucified next to him who begged Jesus to remember him, "Today, you will be with me in paradise" (Luke 23:43).

Part 2: Addiction and Suffering

Addiction is a form of suffering. It is a disease that affects the brain and behavior, causing compulsive drug-seeking and use despite harmful consequences. Addiction is often characterized by physical and emotional pain, as well as social and spiritual consequences.

That's why it is so vital that in addition to its physical and emotional aspects, individuals also take seriously that addiction has a spiritual dimension. Addiction can be seen as a manifestation of spiritual deadness, which is characterized by a sense of disconnection from self, others, and God. Addiction is often driven by a sense of emptiness or lack of purpose that can lead to a search for pleasure or relief through substance use.

According to Luther's theology of the cross, this sense of emptiness and deadness is an opportunity for God's grace to enter into a person's distress and create new life. The cross of Jesus Christ reveals God's forgiveness and grace precisely while suffering and struggling. Therefore, we must pay attention to Luther's theology of the cross as it emphasizes the importance of suffering in the Christian life, not as a punishment or a sign of God's displeasure, but as the place where God meets us with his grace and peace to heal our suffering.

One example from the Bible that helps illustrate that suffering is not a punishment or a sign of God's displeasure is the story of Job. Job is a righteous man who fears God and turns away from evil, but he experiences great suffering and loss, including the deaths of his children, the destruction of his property, and a painful illness. Job's friends suggest that his suffering is a punishment for his sins, but Job maintains his innocence and faith in God.

In the end, God speaks to Job and reveals that his suffering is not a punishment but a test of his faith. Job emerges from his trials with a deeper understanding of God's will and a greater appreciation for the blessings of life. Through his suffering, Job experiences God's grace and learns to trust God's goodness and love. In Job's experience, we see that God can work through our trials to bring about good in our lives.

In addiction recovery, suffering can play a similar role. Recovery involves a process of facing and working through painful emotions and experiences. This process can be difficult and uncomfortable and cause individuals to question whether God has abandoned or cursed them, but it can also be life-changing. Through the experience of suffering, addicts can gain a deeper understanding of themselves and their relationship with God when it is clarified that their suffering is not a punishment from God but a test of faith and an experience intended to deepen their relationship with Jesus, leading them to rely more and more on God's forgiveness and grace.

Luther writes about the life-changing power of suffering in his commentary on Romans 5:4:

> God accepts no one as righteous whom He has not first tested, and He proves him through no other means than through the fire of tribulation... Thus in this testing one comes in no other way than through endurance. And this testing takes place in order that each person may see his own state of mind, that is, that each may know himself, namely, whether he really loves God for the sake of God, which God of course knows even without any testing... [so] the reason why God brings tribulations to men, in order that He might test them, that is, make them approved through endurance. For if God should not test us by tribulation, it would be impossible for any man to be saved.[7]

---

[7] Martin Luther, "Commentary on Romans," in *Luther's Works*, vol. 25, ed. Hilton C. Oswald (Saint Louis: Concordia Publishing House, 1972), 291.

Part 3: The Role of the Cross in Addiction Recovery

Addiction recovery can be seen as a time of renewal of faith and a radical change of life, characterized by a deepening understanding of God's forgiveness and grace for the individual that is pronounced most dramatically when Jesus Christ is crucified for the sin of the world.

According to Luther, the cross is the ultimate symbol of God's forgiveness and grace. Through the cross, God demonstrates his love for humanity, and through the cross, humanity is reconciled to God. In addiction recovery, the cross serves as a powerful reminder of God's grace and forgiveness, even amid suffering and deadness.

Luther's theology of the cross also emphasizes the importance of faith in Christian life. Faith is not just a belief in God but a trust in God's promises and a reliance on God's grace. Faith is essential for addiction recovery, providing the foundation for a new life and hope.

In addiction recovery, faith in Christ Jesus is also a source of strength and guidance. Through faith, addicts can develop a deeper appreciation for the power of God's grace, which strengthens them to bear the burden that accompanies the challenges of addiction. Faith is a source of joy and confidence in the face of adversity. Through faith in Jesus Christ, addicts can develop a deeper sense of hope and trust in God's grace.

To return to the example of Job, Job maintains his faith and trust in God. He says, "Naked I came from my mother's womb, and naked shall I return. The LORD gave, and the LORD has taken away; blessed be the name of the LORD" (Job 1:21). Job's faith allows him to endure his suffering and maintain his confidence in God's goodness and power.

Finally, Luther's theology of the cross also points to the importance of community in the Christian life as the crucified Christ calls into fellowship with him in his Church. Likewise, in addiction recovery, a community of faith and support groups can play a critical role in providing support, accountability, and encouragement in that we "bear one another's burdens and so fulfill the law of Christ," as the apostle Paul writes to the Galatian Christians (Gal 6:2).

Christians are called to support and care for one another, especially in times of difficulty. This is particularly relevant in addiction recovery, where the support of a community of faith and support groups can be crucial for maintaining sobriety and achieving long-term recovery.

In addition to practical support, a community of faith can provide the individual with pastoral care, the mutual consolation and comfort of being supported by other believers, and a sense of belonging and purpose. This is especially relevant when one considers that many addicts struggle with feelings of isolation and disconnection, which can lead to a sense of hopelessness and despair. A community of faith can provide a sense of connection and belonging, which can help to alleviate these feelings and provide a new sense of purpose.

Part 4: From Spiritual Death to Life in God's Grace

The first step in applying Luther's theology of the cross in addiction recovery is to acknowledge spiritual deadness.

Addiction is a manifestation of spiritual deadness, which is characterized by a sense of disconnection from self, others, and a higher power. It is important to acknowledge this deadness rather than trying to hide or deny it.

The second step in applying Luther's theology of the cross in addiction recovery is trust in God's grace. As has been emphasized in the previous two chapters, recovery is not something that can be achieved through willpower or self-effort. Rather, recovery is a process of healing and living a new life made possible through the grace of Jesus Christ.

Luther writes about the importance of trusting in God's grace in his commentary on Galatians 3:23:

> Therefore it is not enough for us to be confined under the Law; for if nothing else were to follow, we would be forced to despair and to die in our sins. But Paul adds that we are confined and restrained under a custodian, the Law, not forever but until Christ, who is the end of the Law (Rom. 10:4). Therefore this terror, humiliation, and custody are not to last forever; they are to last until faith should come. That is, they are for our salvation and for our benefit, so that we who have been terrified by the Law may taste the sweetness of grace, the forgiveness of sins, and deliverance from the Law, sin, and death, which are not acquired by works but are grasped by faith alone.[8]

It is through faith in Christ that we are justified and set free from the bondage of addiction. So, we must trust

---

[8] Martin Luther, "Commentary on Galatians," in *Luther's Works*, vol. 26, ed. Jaroslav Pelikan (Saint Louis: Concordia Publishing House, 1964), 336-337.

in God's grace and rely on his power to bring about renewed faith, a radical change of life, and healing.

The third step in applying Luther's theology of the cross in addiction recovery is to seek support within a community of believers. Recovery is not something that can be undertaken alone. We need the support and encouragement of other believers to trust in God's forgiveness and grace, maintain sobriety, and achieve long-term recovery.

Luther addresses the importance of community support in his commentary on Galatians 6:1 when he writes that,

> when John and James... wanted to call down fire from heaven upon the Samaritans, Christ forbade them, saying: Do you not know what spirit's children you are? The Son of Man did not come to destroy souls but to save them. So, we should give thought, not to how we may destroy but to how we may save the brother who is a sinner.[9]

Christians are called to support and care for one another, especially in times of difficulty. We need the support of a community to stay accountable and to receive the encouragement and guidance we need to maintain sobriety and achieve long-term recovery.

Luther's theology of the cross punctuates the importance of suffering and deadness in the Christian life. In addiction recovery, this theology can provide

---

[9] Martin Luther, "Commentary on Galatians," in *Luther's Works*, vol. 27, ed. Jaroslav Pelikan (Saint Louis: Concordia Publishing House, 1964), 388-389.

a unique perspective for understanding the spiritual dimension of addiction and the opportunity for healing and changing lives. By acknowledging our spiritual deadness, trusting in God's grace, and seeking the support of a community of believers, addicts can find hope and meaning in their struggles and begin the process of recovery.

Moreover, Luther's theology of the cross can help addicts see their struggles in a new light, as an opportunity for a deeper relationship with Jesus Christ and a new life free from the effects of addiction. And though it's true for many addicts, that addiction recovery can be long and difficult, by embracing the theology of the cross addicts can find the strength and courage they need to persevere.

As the apostle Paul writes in Romans 8:18, "For I consider that the sufferings of this present time are not worth comparing with the glory that is to be revealed to us." The apostle is not saying that the present tribulations are insignificant. And he is not saying that our present life is worthless. It is the work of God's hands, after all, and is therefore valuable. Instead, he is speaking of the incomparable glory that is coming at the Last Day. The present tribulations, which do not have the power to destroy us, are to be compared to future glory, which is so great that it is beyond our understanding and can only be grasped at present in faith.

Luther's theology of the cross also highlights the importance of humility and self-denial. Humility and self-denial focus our attention on the need for perseverance and endurance in the face of adversity since addiction recovery can be long and difficult, and there are often setbacks and challenges along the way. But, as the apostle Paul writes in 2 Corinthians 12:9:

> But he said to me, "My grace is sufficient for you, for my power is made perfect in weakness." Therefore, I will boast all the more gladly of my weaknesses, so that the power of Christ may rest upon me.

The apostle Paul directs us to rely on God's grace and power in times of weakness and struggle. By embracing this perspective, addicts can find the strength and courage they need to persevere through the challenges of addiction recovery so that even the struggles and challenges of addiction can ultimately lead to a life of meaning, purpose, and freedom in Christ.

However, this is not a linear path. The addict does not necessarily travel from addiction to sobriety along a demarcated line of recovery. Often, the individual will suffer from thoughts and feelings of wanting to be sober but struggle with perpetual cravings, setbacks, and relapse. This is where Martin Luther's teaching on the Christian as *simul iustus et peccator* can offer the individual encouragement and hope to continue trusting in God and participating in a program of sobriety.

According to Luther, believers are both righteous and sinful at the same time, and they continually struggle with their sinful nature even as they strive to live according to God's will. This teaching has profound implications for addiction recovery, as addicts can find comfort in knowing that their struggles with addiction do not define them completely.

Therefore, in the next chapter, we will explore how Luther's teaching of *simul iustus et peccator* can help addicts in their recovery and how they can find hope and redemption amid their struggles.

Chapter 4

Luther's Formulation of *Simul Iustus et Peccator* and Addiction

...when he kneels at other times and prays
or meditates or tries to achieve a Big-Picture
spiritual understanding of God as he can
understand Him, he feels Nothing—not
nothing, but Nothing, an edgeless blankness
that somehow feels worse than the sort of
unconsidered atheism he Came In with.

—David Foster Wallace, *Infinite Jest*

One of Martin Luther's most profound and impact-
ful teachings was his assertion of the believer in Jesus
Christ as *simul iustus et peccator*, which translates to
"at the same time righteous and sinner." This teaching lies at the heart of Luther's theology and is key to
understanding the Christian life. Luther asserts that
believers are justified, or declared righteous, solely by
faith in Jesus Christ's redemptive work. However, he
also recognizes that believers continue to struggle with
temptation and sin even after experiencing this justification. Thus, this doctrine holds significant implications for individuals in addiction recovery, who face a

lifelong battle against addiction and the persistent lure of temptation.

Luther's teaching of *simul iustus et peccator* acknowledges the complex nature of human existence, particularly for our purposes, as it relates to addiction. On the one hand, individuals in recovery have experienced the transformative power of God's grace and have been declared righteous through faith in Christ. They have also embarked on a program of sobriety, which includes healing and restoration. However, the reality of the ongoing struggle with addiction and temptation persists. The sinful nature within them continues to rear its head, causing them to stumble and falter. It is in this tension between the declaration of righteousness and the ongoing struggle with sin that addicts in recovery find solace and understanding in Luther's teaching.

Understanding oneself as *simul iustus et peccator* offers addicts a theological perspective for comprehending their recovery process. It acknowledges that recovery is not a linear path of instantaneous deliverance from addiction. Instead, it is a lifelong discipline of spiritual maturation, personal change, and continual reliance on God's grace in Jesus Christ for everything. Addicts in recovery recognize that while they have been justified through faith in Christ, they still grapple with the remnants of their addictive patterns and the allure of substances or behaviors that once held them captive.

But Luther's teaching reminds addicts that they are not alone in their struggle. They are part of a broader Christian community, all of whom experience the tension of being simultaneously righteous and sinful. This recognition fosters empathy, compassion, and support among individuals in recovery, as they can sympathize with one another's battles and offer encouragement during shared struggles. The understanding of *simul iustus et peccator* also dispels any notions of judgment or condemnation, as addicts realize that their struggles do not define their worth or standing before God. Instead, their identity is firmly rooted in the righteousness freely declared and imputed to them through faith in Christ.

Moreover, Luther's teaching on *simul iustus et peccator* provides addicts with a realistic approach to their recovery. It acknowledges that recovery is not a destination but a continuous call by God to repentance and renewal. It calls addicts to embrace their ongoing need for the grace of Jesus Christ and to rely on his strength to navigate the challenges of recovery. This understanding encourages individuals in recovery to persevere and not lose hope in the face of setbacks or relapses. They understand that the struggle against addiction is a daily battle, but their righteousness in Christ fuels their determination to press on, to resist temptation, and to strive for a deeper relationship with their Savior continually.

Part 1: The Christian as Simul Iustus Et Peccator

Luther's teaching on *simul iustus et peccator* is rooted in his understanding of justification by faith. He argues that human beings are justified or seen as righteous in the sight of God, not through their good works or merits but solely by faith in Christ. However, even after justification, believers still struggle with sin. Luther explains this paradox in his commentary on Galatians:

For, on the one hand, it is true that we are justified, and that the one thing necessary for us is to know and believe this. On the other hand, we find that we are not yet completely righteous and that we still sin. These two things must be held together, namely, that we are sinners and that we are righteous.[1]

For Luther, the Christian life is a constant struggle between the old Adam, the sinful nature, and the new man in Christ, or the regenerate nature. He writes in his letter to a colleague, Philip Melanchthon:

This life therefore is not righteousness but growth in righteousness, not health but healing, not being but becoming, not rest but exercise. We are not yet what we shall be, but we are growing toward it, the process is not yet finished, but it is going on, this is not the end, but it is the road. All does not yet gleam in glory, but all is being purified.[2]

In other words, believers are not perfect but are constantly dying to sin and being raised anew by God's forgiveness and grace. This constant, daily dying and being reborn is marked by a deepening awareness of one's sinfulness and greater dependence on Christ's

---

[1] Martin Luther, "Commentary on Galatians," in *Luther's Works*, vol. 26, ed. Jaroslav Pelikan (Saint Louis: Concordia Publishing House, 1964), 183.

[2] Martin Luther, "Letter to Philip Melanchthon, August 1, 1521," in *Luther's Works*, vol. 48, ed. Jaroslav Pelikan, Hilton C. Oswald, and Helmut T. Lehmann (Saint Louis: Concordia Publishing House, 1963), 276.

righteousness for comfort and consolation during struggle and afflictions.

Manasseh, for example, is one of the most wicked kings in Judah's history. He worships false gods, builds altars to them in the temple of the Lord, and even sacrifices his children to them. As a result of his evil deeds, God allows him to be captured by the Assyrians and taken into exile (2 Kgs 21:1-8, 2 Chr 33:1-20). However, while in captivity, God repents Manasseh of his sin, and by doing this, God causes Manasseh to pray to him for forgiveness and mercy. God then listens to his prayers and restores Manasseh to his throne in Jerusalem.

After his return, Manasseh completely turns away from his wicked ways and begins to serve the Lord. He removes the idols and altars of false gods, restores the temple of the Lord, and encourages the people to worship the true God. Finally, he walks away from the throne and dedicates his remaining days to caring for the garden in his backyard.

So, Manasseh's story is a powerful example of dying from sin and being raised anew by God. Despite his extreme wickedness, God does not give up on Manasseh. Instead, he allows Manasseh to experience the consequences of his sin, which leads to his repentance and restoration. Through God's grace and mercy, Manasseh is transformed from a wicked king to a faithful servant of God, from a homicidal tyrant to a humble gardener.

Likewise, in the book of the prophet Isaiah, we are shown how even God's faithful preachers can struggle with the temptation to sin. In this passage, Isaiah has a vision of the Lord seated on a throne, surrounded by angels. Overwhelmed by the majesty and holiness of

God, Isaiah cries out, "Woe is me! For I am lost; for I am a man of unclean lips, and I dwell in the midst of a people of unclean lips; for my eyes have seen the King, the LORD of hosts!" (Isa 6:5). Isaiah recognizes that he is a sinner in the presence of a holy God. He is *simul iustus et peccator*, both justified and sinful simultaneously. So, God does not reject Isaiah or leave him in his sin. Instead, one of the angels takes a coal from the altar and touches Isaiah's lips, saying, "Your guilt is taken away, and your sin atoned for" (Isa 6:7).

Through this vision, Isaiah experiences both the reality of his sin and the grace of God's forgiveness. He is justified through God's atonement but remains a sinner in need of God's mercy and grace. This experience shapes Isaiah's prophetic ministry, as he becomes a voice for God's justice and mercy to sinful people. Therefore, Isaiah's vision illustrates the tension between justification and sinfulness at the heart of Luther's teaching that a Christian is *simul iustus et peccator*. We are both justified through faith in Christ and remain sinners needing God's ongoing grace and forgiveness.

Thus, the teaching about *simul iustus et peccator* has powerful implications for addicts in recovery. Addiction is a disease that affects not only the body but also the mind, spirit, and relationships. It is a disease that can be overcome by the grace of Christ that simultaneously requires a lifelong commitment to sobriety in an ever-deepening dependence on Christ Jesus. Luther's teaching on *simul iustus et peccator* can help addicts understand and navigate the recovery process in several ways.

Part 2: Recognizing One's Own Sinfulness & Dependence on Christ's Righteousness

The first step in the recovery process is recognizing one's sinfulness and need for forgiveness and healing. Luther's teaching on *simul iustus et peccator* emphasizes the reality of human sinfulness and the ongoing struggle against temptation and addiction. This teaching can help addicts come to terms with their spiritual deadness and begin the process of actual healing from the ravages of addiction.

In his commentary on Romans, Luther writes:

> We are all thieves, and every one of us deserves the gallows. Christ, however, took upon Himself the form of a sinner and bore the punishment of sin, not for His own sins but for ours. In this way, He blotted out the handwriting which was against us and nailed it to the cross.[3]

From this, we can learn to acknowledge, along with the apostle Paul, that sin is a universal affliction. But held in tension with Christ's sacrifice for sinners, it offers hope to addicts who feel trapped in their addiction. By confessing their sinfulness and turning to Christ for forgiveness and healing, God begins to break free the addict from the dynamic of their addiction and move them towards recovery.

We witness this in the Gospel of John, when the scribes and Pharisees bring a woman before Jesus,

---

[3] Martin Luther, "Romans Commentary," in *Luther's Works*, vol. 25, ed. Jaroslav Pelikan (Saint Louis: Concordia Publishing House, 1963), 301-2.

accusing her of adultery and demanding that she be stoned, as was the punishment under Jewish law. However, Jesus responds, "Let him who is without sin among you be the first to throw a stone at her" (John 8:7). The accusers, realizing their sinfulness, drop their stones and walk away. Jesus then tells the woman, "Neither do I condemn you; go, and from now on sin no more" (John 8:11). This exchange illustrates humanity's sinfulness and the forgiveness and mercy available through Jesus Christ.

In these and other accounts in the gospels, Jesus emphasizes the need for repentance and faith as the way to salvation. He also emphasizes the importance of showing mercy and forgiveness to others, as we have received mercy and forgiveness from God. These examples show how the old proverb that "we are all thieves, and every one of us deserves the gallows" is countered by the grace and forgiveness available through Jesus Christ.

The second aspect of Luther's teaching on *simul iustus et peccator* that can help addicts in recovery is the idea of dependence on Christ's righteousness. Addiction is an affliction that often stems from a deep sense of shame, guilt, and self-loathing. Addicts may feel that they are beyond redemption or that they are unworthy of God's love and acceptance. Luther's teaching emphasizes that justification and righteousness come not from our efforts but from faith in Christ. In his commentary on Galatians, Luther writes:

> For faith does not bring righteousness because it contributes anything to our salvation, but because it receives the promise which is offered in the promise

of the Gospel, namely, the forgiveness of sins and justification.[4]

By depending on Christ's righteousness and not their own, addicts can begin to break free from the cycle of shame and self-loathing that often accompanies addiction. Instead, they can find hope in the promise of forgiveness and justification through faith in Jesus Christ.

Examples of this can be found in the Book of Judges, in the stories of Gideon and Samson. God chose Gideon to deliver Israel from the Midianites. Despite his doubts and fears, Gideon demonstrates faith in God's promise to be with him and give him victory. In Judges 6:14-16, the Angel of the Lord says to Gideon:

> "Go in this might of yours and save Israel from the hand of Midian; do not I send you?" And [Gideon] said to him, "Please, Lord, how can I save Israel? Behold, my clan is the weakest in Manasseh, and I am the least in my father's house." And the LORD said to him, "But I will be with you, and you shall strike the Midianites as one man."

Through faith in God's promise to be with him, Gideon can overcome his doubts and fears and ultimately deliver Israel from their oppressors.

God also chooses Samson to deliver Israel from their enemies, the Philistines. Despite his flaws and weaknesses, Samson demonstrates faith in God's promise to

---

[4] Martin Luther, "Commentary on Galatians," in *Luther's Works*, vol. 26, ed. Jaroslav Pelikan, (Saint Louis: Concordia Publishing House, 1963), 121.

be with him and strengthen him. In Judges 16:28-30, we read:

> Then Samson called to the LORD and said, "O Lord GOD, please remember me and please strengthen me only this once, O God, that I may be avenged on the Philistines for my two eyes." And Samson grasped the two middle pillars on which the house rested, and he leaned his weight against them, his right hand on the one and his left hand on the other. And Samson said, "Let me die with the Philistines." Then he bowed with all his strength, and the house fell upon the lords and upon all the people who were in it. So the dead whom he killed at his death were more than those whom he had killed during his life.

As with Gideon, through faith in God's promise to give him strength, Samson can accomplish God's purposes and deliver Israel from their enemies even in his weakened state.

In both examples, we see individuals who find hope in the promise of God's presence and power despite their weaknesses and limitations. They can overcome their fears and doubts through faith in God's promises and accomplish great things for God's kingdom.

Part 3: Relying on Christ's Strength & Grace to Persevere

The final aspect of Luther's teaching on *simul iustus et peccator* that can help addicts in recovery is perseverance in the struggle against sin and addiction. Recovery is a lifelong discipline, and addicts will inevitably face setbacks, temptations, and relapses along the way. Luther's teaching emphasizes the ongoing struggle between the old Adam—our sinful nature—and the new man in Christ—our regenerate nature—and the need to persevere in faith. In his commentary on Romans, Luther writes:

> The righteousness of faith, then, is not only present, but it is growing and increasing in believers as they fight against sin and temptation. For as long as we live in this flesh, we will always have the old Adam to contend with. But by faith, we can put to death the deeds of the flesh and walk in newness of life.[5]

By understanding the ongoing struggle against sin and addiction and by relying on Christ's strength and grace to persevere, addicts can find the courage and determination to continue on the path of recovery.

Again, we can turn to the gospels for examples illustrating this final point. In the story of the paralytic in Mark 2:1-12, a group of men bring their paralyzed friend to Jesus for healing. Jesus forgives the man's sins, and when questioned by the religious leaders, he says, "Which is easier, to say to the paralytic, 'Your sins are forgiven,' or to say, 'Rise, take up your bed and walk'?" (Mark 2:9). Jesus then tells the man to get up and walk, demonstrating the interconnectedness of physical and spiritual healing. This story shows that Jesus cares about our physical and spiritual well-being

---

[5] Martin Luther, "Romans Commentary," in *Luther's Works*, vol. 25, ed. Jaroslav Pelikan, (Saint Louis; Concordia Publishing House, 1963), 117.

and will not allow sin to be a barrier to his attending to either one.

Next, in the events leading up to Jesus' crucifixion, Peter denies knowing Jesus three times (Matt 26:69-75). After the third denial, he weeps bitterly, remembering Jesus' previous promise that he would deny Jesus three times before the rooster crowed. This story illustrates the human tendency to fall into sin, even for those closest to Jesus, and the importance of repentance and forgiveness in restoring broken relationships with God.

Finally, in the example of the two men crucified with Jesus, one of the criminals mocks Jesus, but the other rebukes him and asks Jesus to remember him when he comes into his kingdom. Jesus responds, "Truly I tell you, today you will be with me in Paradise" (Luke 23:39-43). This story highlights the power of repentance and faith, even at the last moment of a person's life. The thief on the cross acknowledges his sinfulness and asks for forgiveness, and Jesus offers him eternal life. This example shows how even in a person's near-death state, there is still hope for redemption through faith in Christ.

The doctrine of *simul iustus et peccator* offers a compelling perspective for understanding the Christian life that considers the struggles of addiction and recovery. By recognizing that we are both righteous and sinful at the same time - sinful in ourselves but declared righteous in Christ Jesus by faith - we can avoid the pitfalls of legalism and despair and instead find hope and strength in the grace of God. We are saints and sinners at the same time, and we will be until the day we die. But by faith in Christ, we can trust that he will put to death our reliance on our efforts and works so that we may walk with him in the newness of life.

For addicts in recovery, the doctrine of *simul iustus et peccator* offers a way to embrace the reality of their past sins and current struggles while also finding hope in the promise of forgiveness and justification through faith in Jesus Christ. By recognizing that we are not yet what we shall be but are growing toward it, addicts can take comfort in the fact that recovery is a process, not a destination. By relying on the work of Jesus Christ for their ultimate good, they are given the strength to continue in repentance, faith, and healing.

Ultimately, the doctrine of *simul iustus et peccator* offers a way to hold together the tension between our sinfulness and the righteousness that is ours through faith in Jesus Christ, who is with us in our struggles, giving us hope, forgiving our past sins and leading us towards the reward of eternal life. By embracing this paradoxical reality, we can find the freedom and joy that comes from living in the grace of God, as Paul wrote in Romans 7:24-25, "Wretched man that I am! Who will deliver me from this body of death? Thanks be to God through Jesus Christ our Lord! So then, I myself serve the law of God with my mind, but with my flesh I serve the law of sin."

Part 4: Put to Death in Sin, Raised to New Life in Faith

Once one embraces the paradox that we are simultaneously sinful in ourselves and declared righteous through faith in Christ, we begin to grasp how recovery is, in many ways, a mirror of the Christian life, as believers are called to put to death the power of sin and be raised to new life in Christ. In Romans 6:6, the apostle Paul writes, "We know that our old self was crucified with him in order that the body of sin might be brought to nothing, so that we would no longer be enslaved to sin."

This verse emphasizes the necessity of crucifying the old self - as manifested in addiction - and allowing it to be rendered powerless. Recovery demands a change of heart and a new willingness to confront and dismantle the destructive patterns that underlie addiction, acknowledging the need for radical transformation that only God can affect. Luther aptly describes this experience, stating:

> The Old Adam in us should by daily contrition and repentance be drowned and die with all sins and evil desires, and that a new man should daily emerge and arise to live before God in righteousness and purity forever.[6]

The daily baptism that Luther refers to encompasses the ongoing discipline of recovery. It involves continuous activity by God, putting our sin to death, including the power of addiction, and raising us to new life in faith in Christ. Each day then presents an opportunity to renew one's commitment to sobriety, confront the underlying

---

[6] Martin Luther, "The Large Catechism," in *The Book of Concord: The Confessions of the Evangelical Lutheran Church*, ed. Robert Kolb and Timothy J. Wengert (Minneapolis: Fortress Press, 2000), 360.

wounds and struggles that fuel addiction, and cling to the sobering power of God's grace.

Biblical examples illuminate this paradox, such as the life of the apostle Paul. Before his conversion, Paul was a zealous persecutor of Christians. However, through a dramatic encounter with Christ on the road to Damascus, he was converted and became one of the most influential figures in the early Christian movement (Acts 9:1-31).

In his letter to the Galatians, Paul writes, "I have been crucified with Christ. It is no longer I who live, but Christ who lives in me" (Gal 2:20). This profound statement encapsulates the essence of recovery. Jesus defeats the old self, with its destructive habits and patterns, by coming to live with us and work for our good. It is through this defeat, forced surrender, and a new relationship with Jesus Christ that individuals in recovery can experience a true change of heart and a liberation from the bondage of addiction.

Both Paul and Luther acknowledge the reality of our fallen nature and the ongoing battle with sin. However, they also affirm the power of God's grace and the work of the Holy Spirit to kill sin in us so that we can be raised anew to walk with Jesus Christ in his forgiveness and grace. As Luther beautifully puts it, "God does not save those who are only imaginary sinners. Be a sinner and sin boldly, but believe and rejoice in Christ even more boldly."[7] This paradoxical statement

---

[7] "Let Your Sins Be Strong: A Letter from Luther to Melanchthon: Letter no. 99, 1 August 1521: From Wartburg Castle," trans. by Erika Bullmann Flores, http://www.ctsfw.net/media/pdfs/LutherToMelanchthon.pdf.

emphasizes the need to recognize that in ourselves, we are dead men walking. Yet, our ultimate trust in Christ's redeeming work means death doesn't get the final word about our eternal destiny.

Therefore, recovery is not an activity embarked upon in isolation; it is a daily clinging to God's grace. Like a drop of water clings to the side of a pitcher, we cling to God as he constantly drowns our weaknesses and struggles to raise us in the newness of life to walk with Jesus in righteousness, innocence, and blessedness forever. It is in this that we are free to admit with all boldness and confidence that our identity is found in Christ, not in our past choices, behaviors, or addictions.

And as the apostle Paul writes in 2 Corinthians 5:17, "Therefore, if anyone is in Christ, he is a new creation. The old has passed away; behold, the new has come." This truth offers hope and encouragement to those in recovery, reminding them that they are not defined by their past or their addiction but by their new life in Christ.

So, our clinging to God's grace is a recognition that we cannot overcome addiction in our strength. We acknowledge our desperate need for God's intervention and rely on his power to change us. As Luther states, "This life, therefore, is not godliness but the process of becoming godly, not health but getting well, not being but becoming, not rest but exercise."[8] Recovery, therefore, is not a destination but a daily experience of

---

[8] Martin Luther, "Defense and Explanation of All the Articles," in *Luther's Works*, vol. 32: Career of the Reformer II, ed. George W. Forell and Helmut T. Lehman (Minneapolis: Fortress Press, 1958), 24.

healing and becoming. It is an ongoing exercise of faith, entrusting ourselves to the work of God in our lives.

In the discipline of recovery, we confront the reality that our past choices, behaviors, and addictions do not define us. We are not trapped by our choices or the chains that once bound us. Instead, our identity is found in Jesus Christ, who has redeemed and set us free from our captivity to addiction. This recognition aligns with Luther's understanding of the Christian life as a daily dying and rising. The old self, characterized by spiritual deadness within addiction, has passed away. In its place, a new creation emerges, a person changed by the grace of Christ, clothed in his righteousness, and called to walk in newness of life with Jesus all the days of their life.

And as has been previously stated, their past struggles or failures no longer define them, but their present reality as new creations in Christ. Through the power of Christ's death and resurrection, they have been set free from the grip of addiction and are now strengthened to live with their God and Savior in righteousness and purity.

In embracing the reality of living as *simul iustus et peccator,* individuals in recovery find hope and encouragement. They understand that the daily struggle with addiction does not disqualify them from God's forgiveness and grace. Rather, it serves as a reminder of their ongoing need for God's good work in their lives. Then, recovery becomes a testament to the power of Christ's death and resurrection, as he continuously puts to death the old self and the power of sin and raises us to a new life so that we can walk with him into the resurrection to eternal life.

Chapter 5

Luther's Teachings on Election and the Sacraments and Addiction

The pursuit of alcohol becomes a
distorted symbol of reward, a numbing
agent that temporarily satisfies their longing
for a better life.

—Rove Monteux,
What is Wrong with Society Today

By delving into Martin Luther's teaching on the importance of God's election and the significance of the sacraments in the lives of Christians, we uncover a theological scaffolding that supports individuals grappling with addiction.[1] Luther's teachings offer a powerful message of hope and solace for those caught in the throes of addiction, providing them with a divine

---

[1] The sacraments are literally, "promises which have signs attached to them," as Luther writes in "The Babylonian Captivity of the Church," in *Luther's Works*, vol. 36, edited by Abdul Ross Wentz and Helmut T. Lehmann (Minneapolis: Fortress Press, 1959), 124-126.

choice that opens a door to redemption and healing for them.

Luther forcefully advocates for the biblical teaching of election, testified to by the gospel writer John, for example, who records Jesus saying, "You did not choose me, but I chose you and appointed you that you should go and bear fruit and that your fruit should abide, so that whatever you ask the Father in my name, he may give it to you" (John 15:16). Based on John's gospel and numerous other biblical texts, Luther asserts that God, in his infinite wisdom and mercy, chooses individuals for salvation based on his grace alone rather than any merit or worthiness on their part. For individuals burdened by addiction, this teaching carries immense significance. It assures them that their past mistakes or current struggles do not determine their worth and identity. Instead, their comfort is located in knowing that God's love and acceptance are unconditional and that he has specifically chosen them through Jesus' bloody suffering and death on the cross.

Furthermore, Luther's formulation of election highlights the role of the sacraments as tangible, graspable means of receiving God's forgiveness and grace.[2] The sacraments, particularly baptism and the Lord's Supper hold great significance for Luther. Baptism is the washing away of sin through the action of God's Word and the Holy Spirit and an initiation into the community of believers, while the Lord's Supper declares the

---

[2] Another way to conceive of the sacraments of baptism and the Lord's Supper is that they are visible words that deliver God's promises of forgiveness, new life, and eternal life.

ongoing nourishment and sustenance of the believer's faith through the eating of Jesus' body and the drinking of Jesus' blood, "which is poured out for many for the forgiveness of sins" (Matt 26:28).

So, for individuals grappling with addiction, these sacraments serve as powerful reminders of God's choosing them to be not just his chosen people but his children who daily experience renewal and restoration through his promises of forgiveness, life, and salvation that are made graspable in the sacraments. The sacraments provide a tangible connection to God's grace, reinforcing the message that forgiveness and healing are available to all who seek them.

In their recovery, individuals struggling with addiction can find solace in Luther's theology through the guidance of the Holy Spirit. Luther emphasizes the role of the Holy Spirit as the one who empowers and transforms believers, strengthening them to overcome their struggles and live a new life with Jesus Christ. Recognizing the Holy Spirit's presence and active work in their lives brings hope and strength to those battling addiction, assuring them that they do not face their challenges alone. The Holy Spirit's guidance and support provide the necessary fortitude and resilience to overcome addiction's grip and embrace a life of freedom and wholeness.

Ultimately, Luther's teachings on God's election and the sacraments offer a compelling message of God's unmerited forgiveness and grace, which profoundly speaks to the hearts of individuals struggling with addiction. It reminds them that their past does not define them and that God loves and chooses them, regardless of their struggles. Through the graspable

promise of God's forgiveness and grace in the sacraments and the guidance of the Holy Spirit, those facing
addiction can find hope, restoration, and a renewed
sense of purpose as they are plunged into a new life of
recovery and healing.

Part 1: The Power of God's Grace and Forgiveness

At the core of Martin Luther's theology lies a provocative
belief in God's boundless grace and forgiveness. Luther
understands that human beings are inherently sinful
and fall far short of God's standard for righteousness.
However, he emphasizes that the depths of our struggles
or the gravity of our sins do not limit God's mercy and
forgiveness. In his 1518 *Heidelberg Disputation*, Luther
boldly proclaimed, "The love of God does not find, but
creates, that which is pleasing to it."[3]

But how could God take sinners who fall short of
his righteousness and make something lovable out of
them? Luther's intention is not to encourage a lifestyle
of unrepentant sin as if our continual, unrepentant sin
endears us to God. Rather, he seeks to convey the depth
of God's love and mercy that surpasses our understanding. Luther recognizes that if we dwell solely on our sins,
real or imagined, and allow guilt and shame to paralyze
us, we will be unable to fully embrace the grace and
forgiveness that God freely gives us through his efforts
to make us worthy of his love.

---

[3] Martin Luther, "The Heidelberg Disputation," in *Luther's
Works*, vol. 31: Career of the Reformer I, ed. Harold J. Grimm
(Saint Louis: Concordia Publishing House, 1957), 41.

Luther's words remind us that God's love and forgiveness are not contingent upon our efforts to be righteous. Instead, it is through faith in Christ and God's doing something impossible for us to accomplish on our own that we find true healing and restoration. That means that the Holy Spirit, working through preachers and the sacraments, becomes the vehicle through which God's divine grace is imputed to individuals, paving the way for a changed heart and a renewal of life.

That's why, in Luther's theology, the sacraments play a significant role in the reception of the grace of Christ. Baptism, for instance, is seen as a powerful act of the Holy Spirit that kills the old sinful self and raises a new life, a sinner declared a saint through faith in Christ. Through this tangible promise, individuals are cleansed of their sins and united with Christ, becoming partakers in his redemptive work. Luther writes in his Large Catechism that baptism "is nothing else than the slaying of the old Adam and the resurrection of the new creature, both of which must continue in us our whole life long."[4]

Similarly, the sacrament of the Lord's Supper, also known as Holy Communion, is a tangible, graspable reception of the body and blood of Christ. By partaking in this sacrament, believers are nourished spiritually, receiving the forgiveness of sins, new life, and eternal salvation. Again, in the Large Catechism, Luther asserts, "For this reason [Jesus] bids me eat and drink,

---

[4] Martin Luther, "The Large Catechism," in *The Book of Concord: The Confessions of the Evangelical Lutheran Church*, ed. Robert Kolb and Timothy J. Wengert (Minneapolis: Fortress Press, 2000), 465.

that it may be mine and do me good as a sure pledge and sign - indeed, as the very gift he has provided for me against my sins, death, and all evils."[5]

Through the Holy Spirit's preachers and the sacraments, individuals are constantly reminded that God's grace knows no limits. There is no sin too great, no struggle too overwhelming that God's grace and mercy cannot overcome it. Luther's theology, therefore, provides a profound reassurance to those burdened by addiction, affirming that they are not abandoned or condemned by God but instead called to boldly believe and rejoice in Christ's redemptive work.

For example, in Joshua 2:1-21 and 6:22-25, we learn about Rahab. Rahab is a prostitute living in the city of Jericho, a place known for its idolatry and wickedness. Yet, when the Israelite spies enter Jericho, Rahab protects them and confesses her faith in the God of Israel. As a result, God spared Rahab and her family during the conquest of Jericho. Rahab later becomes part of the lineage of Jesus Christ, exemplifying for generation after generation how God's mercy extends to the most unlikely individuals.

Likewise, in John 4:1-12, Jesus speaks with a Samaritan woman; the result is the same for her as for Rahab. The Samaritan woman Jesus speaks to by a well is an outcast, known for her sinful lifestyle and failed marriages. When Jesus engages her in conversation, he reveals her past and offers her the living water of eternal life. Through his compassion and grace, the Samaritan woman experiences a profound change. She becomes an evangelist, sharing the Good News with her community,

---

[5] Ibid., 469.

and through her preaching, many others are converted and believe that Jesus is their Savior, too.

By understanding and clinging to the same boundless grace and forgiveness that God extends to those two women, individuals in addiction and those in recovery can find the courage to confront their sins honestly and receive God's work for them for what it is, a gift freely given on account of Jesus Christ. They can find hope in the assurance that their struggles do not define their worth or separate them from God's love. Rather, they are invited to approach God's throne of grace with boldness, confident that God's mercy and forgiveness are freely available to all who turn to Christ Jesus in faith.

Luther's theology of God's boundless grace and forgiveness, reinforced by the Holy Spirit's preachers and the sacraments, offers hope for those navigating the complex terrain of addiction and recovery. It illuminates the path to healing and restoration, reminding individuals that no matter how deeply they have fallen, God's mercy extends further still. Through faith in Christ and the reception of God's grace, addicts and those in recovery experience the profound liberation that brings freedom from the chains of addiction and opens the door to a renewed life of purpose and joy.

Thus, in Luther's theology, the stress put on God's boundless grace and forgiveness does not diminish the seriousness of sin. Rather, it highlights the incomparable magnitude of God's love and mercy in Jesus Christ. Luther understands that the weight of guilt and shame can be overwhelming for those struggling with addiction. He recognizes that individuals might question whether they deserve God's forgiveness and doubt their sins can ever be absolved.

However, Luther's theology is a powerful reminder that God's grace is not earned but freely given. It is not contingent upon our efforts to be righteous or deserving. Rather, it is rooted in the sacrificial work of Jesus Christ on the cross, where he bears the weight of our sins and offers redemption to all who believe in him.

We see this most radically in the account of the Philippian jailer in Acts 16:16-40. While Paul and Silas are imprisoned in Philippi, an earthquake shakes the prison, opening the doors and loosening the prisoners' chains. Fearing that the prisoners have escaped and he will suffer the consequences, the jailer is about to take his own life when Paul calls out to him, assuring him that they are all still present. Moved by this display of supernatural power and compassion, the jailer asks Paul and Silas, "Sirs, what must I do to be saved?" They respond, "Believe in the Lord Jesus, and you will be saved, you and your household." The jailer and his household immediately believe and are baptized, emphasizing that salvation is not attained through personal efforts or rituals but through faith in Jesus Christ alone.

This understanding of God's grace encourages and strengthens individuals struggling with addiction to pray to God for salvation with honesty and humility. They can lay their burdens at the feet of Christ, trusting in his power to forgive and restore. Luther's theology, therefore, invites individuals to recognize that their sinfulness does not disqualify them from God's love but rather catalyzes the depth of his forgiveness and grace.

And by embracing this theological perspective, addicts and those in recovery will find the freedom to acknowledge their spiritual deadness without being defined by it. They are instead set free by God's forgiveness to confront their addiction with courage and seek the necessary support and resources for their continued recovery and healing. Rather than being overwhelmed by guilt and shame, they can cling to the promise of God's forgiveness and draw strength from the knowledge that their worth is not determined by their struggles but by the immeasurable love of their Heavenly Father.

Part 2: The Assurance of God's Election

Luther's teaching on election offers a radical message of hope and encouragement for those grappling with addiction. Throughout his works, Luther emphasizes that God's choice to justify sinners extends to all individuals, regardless of their past decisions or present struggles. This liberating message assures addicts and those in recovery that their addiction does not define their identity; rather, their identity is defined by God's loving and intentional choice.

In the depths of addiction, individuals often face overwhelming feelings of guilt, shame, and despair. They may struggle with a sense of worthlessness, believing that their addiction defines not only their life but their entire being. However, Luther's teaching on election provides a life-changing perspective, assuring them that their true identity lies in God's gracious choice to love and redeem them through the life, death, and resurrection of Jesus Christ.

By turning their attention to the cross of Christ, individuals grappling with addiction can find comfort and solace. The cross is the ultimate, one-time-for-all-time expression of God's forgiveness and grace, as

Jesus willingly took the weight of humanity's sins upon himself. It is at the cross that the power of addiction is confronted and overcome, as Christ's sacrifice opens the way to redemption and restoration.

Understanding that they are loved and chosen by God, even in their weakest moments, is a source of intense comfort and strength for individuals amid addiction and recovery. Luther's teaching on election assures them that their struggles do not define their worth or determine their ultimate destiny. Rather, they are held securely in the embrace of God's unwavering love and purpose, which is to "bring good news to the poor… to bind up the brokenhearted, to proclaim liberty to the captives, and the opening of the prison to those who are bound," as the prophet declares (Isa 61:1).

Consider the story of Jonah, God's preacher who is ordered to go to the city of Nineveh and proclaim a message of judgment and repentance. However, Jonah rebels because Nineveh is an enemy of Israel. The Ninevites are cruel, ruthless people who prey upon Jonah and his people. So, he attempts to flee from God's command by boarding a ship heading in the opposite direction. But, after being swallowed by a great fish, Jonah is repented by God and compelled to carry out his mission. Then, to Jonah's surprise, the people of Nineveh, known for their wickedness, respond to Jonah's message by repenting of their evil ways. God, in his mercy, forgives the people of Nineveh and relents from bringing destruction upon them. Thus, Jonah's story exemplifies God's election of sinners and the assurance of forgiveness and redemption, even for those who seem far from him.

So, by embracing their chosenness, individuals in recovery find the courage to face their past, confront their addiction, and pursue a life of healing and whole-ness. They can find hope in knowing that God's forgive-ness and grace are not conditional upon their ability to overcome addiction on their own. Rather, they can trust that God's love is steadfast and always with them in their trials.

Moreover, by being set free from constant worry about how God views them, individuals in recovery from addiction can wholeheartedly embrace a new life characterized by gratitude and humility. Trusting that their redemption is solely a result of God's unmerited favor in Jesus Christ, they are released from the heavy burden of self-reliance and self-condemnation. Instead of striving to earn their worth or prove their righteous-ness, they can rest assured of God's forgiveness and grace.

Part 3: Spreading The Good News of Grace and Recovery

This newfound freedom from self-condemnation lib-erates recovering addicts to announce forgiveness and grace to others. They no longer need to dwell on their past choices or define themselves by their failures. Instead, they can gratefully acknowledge that they were dead in sin, that Jesus came to them and rescued them, and as a consequence, they have been renewed by the life-changing proclamation of forgiveness in the name of Jesus Christ.

Take, again, the example of St. Paul. Paul, also known as Saul of Tarsus, was a Pharisee (a sect of Judaism well-known for their strict adherence to Mosaic law) and persecutor of early Christians. However, his life takes a dramatic turn when he encounters Jesus on the road to Damascus. Blinded by a bright light and confronted by the risen Christ, Paul experiences a radical conversion. Through this encounter, his error is revealed to him, and from then on, he confesses Jesus as the Son of God.

After his conversion, Paul also became one of history's most prolific and influential Christian missionaries. Filled with vigor and passion, he travels extensively, preaching the Gospel of Jesus Christ, planting churches, and nurturing the faith of believers. His letters, which make up a significant portion of the New Testament, are a testament to his deep reverence for the Gospel and his commitment to sharing it with others.

God worked through Paul's preaching and teaching to impact countless lives during his ministry and for generations to come. He fearlessly proclaimed the message of salvation through Jesus Christ, spotlighting the sufficiency of Christ's sacrifice and the life-changing power of his grace. Likewise, Paul's missionary journeys, imprisonment, and eventual martyrdom are a testament to God's unwavering commitment to bring the Gospel of Jesus Christ to all people.

In the same way, Jesus also sends out recovering addicts in the power of the Holy Spirit to announce forgiveness and grace to others within the recovery community. Because they understand the struggles and setbacks that accompany the process of recovery, they are quick to offer support, empathy, and encouragement. More importantly, by experiencing the depth of God's forgiveness and grace, they become ambassadors of Jesus' forgiveness, acting as instruments of the Holy

Spirit who fosters a culture of compassion and forgiveness within the recovery community.

By declaring forgiveness and grace in Jesus' name, individuals in recovery participate in creating an atmosphere where judgment and condemnation are replaced with consolation and compassion. The Holy Spirit makes them beacons of hope for others still on the path to healing, sharing their own experiences and offering guidance, support, prayers, and encouragement. In this way, the recovery community becomes a haven where individuals are encouraged to be authentic and vulnerable, knowing they will be met with kindness and God's unconditional forgiveness.

Embracing a posture of gratitude and humility in this way not only transforms the lives of recovering addicts but also has a profound impact on the broader community. As the Holy Spirit works through them, bringing God's grace and forgiveness into their own lives, they witness the life-changing power of Jesus Christ's redemptive work. Their testimonies about God's free grace and election serve as a beacon of hope for those who are still trapped in the grip of addiction, inspiring them to seek the same freedom and restoration.

Part 3: God's Election, Vocation, and Addiction Recovery

Finally, Luther's teaching on God's election also helps us better understand the purpose and goal of our lives regarding recovery. When it is announced to us by God's preachers that we are chosen in Christ for salvation, the same proclamation provides a meaningful framework for understanding addiction recovery in the context of what has been previously discussed. The Christian doctrine of election reminds individuals grappling with addiction that they are chosen and loved by God, irrespective of their past choices or current struggles. This understanding instills a profound sense of hope and purpose in the process of recovery.

In Luther's theology, election is not solely a matter of individual salvation but also a calling to live out one's faith in the world. This calling, known as vocation, emphasizes that every believer has a unique role and purpose in God's redemptive plan. Applying this perspective to addiction recovery, individuals come to appreciate that their struggle with addiction is not an obstacle to their vocation but rather an opportunity for maturation in faith, personal change, and service to others. As Luther writes,

> In God's sight, it is faith that makes a person holy; it alone serves God, while our works serve people. Here you have every blessing, protection, and shelter under the Lord, and, what is more, a joyful conscience and a gracious God who will reward you a hundredfold.[6]

And since it cannot be stressed enough, within the context of addiction recovery, the doctrine of election assures individuals that their addiction does not define their identity but by Jesus' loving choice, as he says, "You did not choose me, but I chose you..." (John 15:16). This profound truth helps to combat

---

[6] Ibid., 406-407.

feelings of shame, guilt, and unworthiness that often accompany addiction, freeing individuals to embrace their inherent worth as children of God.

Moreover, the reality of their God-given vocation strengthens individuals in recovery to see their sobriety as an integral part of their calling in life. Their struggle with addiction becomes a catalyst for deeper self-reflection, spiritual maturation, and personal change. They can use their own experiences and lessons to help others still trapped in addiction, thus fulfilling their vocation as instruments of God's healing and grace.

In the Book of Ruth, for example, Naomi, who is widowed and childless, decides to return to her homeland of Bethlehem. She encourages her daughters-in-law, Ruth and Orpah, to remain in Moab and find new husbands. Orpah eventually chooses to stay, but Ruth clings to Naomi, uttering one of the most famous declarations of loyalty in the Bible: "Do not urge me to leave you or to return from following you. For where you go I will go, and where you lodge I will lodge. Your people shall be my people, and your God my God" (Ruth 1:16).

Ruth's unwavering commitment to Naomi demonstrates her vocation, a calling that arises from God's love for both women. So, despite the challenges and uncertainties that lie ahead, God continues to strengthen Ruth, keeping steadfast in her determination to support and encourage Naomi.

Upon arriving in Bethlehem, Ruth takes on the humble task of gleaning in the fields to provide for herself and Naomi. Here, she encounters Boaz, a relative of Naomi's late husband. Boaz shows kindness and favor towards Ruth, allowing her to glean in his fields and ensuring her safety and provision.

As the story unfolds, it becomes evident that Ruth's vocation extends beyond mere survival. Boaz recognizes her exceptional character and her sacrificial love for Naomi. He admires her integrity and willingness to embrace her newfound faith and community. Then, Boaz becomes instrumental in God's bringing about redemption and restoration for Ruth and Naomi.

Eventually, Boaz marries Ruth, and they have a son named Obed. Through this union, Ruth's vocation extends beyond herself and Naomi to become a source of blessing for the entire nation. Obed would later become the grandfather of King David, establishing Ruth as an ancestor of Jesus Christ.

This combination of God's election and vocation, which eventually leads to the birth of our Savior, offers a powerful perspective for us on addiction recovery. In the story of Ruth, individuals can read that their recovery is not solely about their well-being but also about their calling to be instruments of God in the world. Their liberation from addiction then becomes a testimony to the life-changing power of Jesus' grace and mercy, inspiring hope in others who are still bound by the chains of addiction.

This understanding also fosters a sense of responsibility and accountability in the recovery process. Individuals acknowledge that they have been entrusted with the gifts of the Holy Spirit and that their path toward wholeness is not solely for their benefit but also for the betterment of others. This recognition compels them to engage in ongoing participation in a community of believers, seeking support from a pastor or other brothers and sisters in Christ and actively participating in a recovery community, offering support, encouragement, and compassion to fellow strugglers. As Luther notes in his exposition of Psalm 147, "Unless God creates with His Word, all our work and effort is for nothing... 'His Word,' not our hand; "His Word," not "our technique," makes and accomplishes all things."[7]

Additionally, the understanding of God's election and vocation provides individuals in recovery with a solid foundation for sustaining their sobriety. Assured that they are chosen and called into a relationship with Jesus Christ, they can rely on him for strength, guidance, and resilience, trusting that the Holy Spirit will navigate them through the challenges and temptations they may encounter on their path to sobriety, trusting that no matter which path they're on, God is guiding and leading them into the company of angels, archangels, and all the company of heaven in the resurrection to eternal life.

So, through the proclamation that they are chosen and loved by God and with the assistance of Martin Luther's theology, individuals in recovery can find hope, strength, and purpose in their sobriety. They are liberated to recognize that their recovery is not separate from their calling but an integral part of it, as they become vessels of God's forgiveness and grace. This understanding then strengthens individuals in faith

---

[7] Martin Luther, "Commentary on Psalm 147," in *Luther's Works*, vol. 14, ed. Jaroslav Pelikan and Helmut T. Lehmann. (Saint Louis: Concordia Publishing House, 1958), 124-125.

to embrace their identity as beloved children of our
Heavenly Father, who are called to rely on the sustaining power of his love and guidance in Jesus Christ all
the days of their lives.

Postscript

What began as a recognition of the paradox inherent in seeking recognition for our achievements transforms into a profound realization that recovery, in its truest sense, defies the boundaries of human attainment. As we conclude this exploration, we stand at the threshold of a revelation—an understanding that the elusive prize is not found in the victory over addiction but in the daily acknowledgment of our dependence on God's grace and mercy.

The winding path we've traversed echoes the rhythm of heartfelt prayer, each step invoking grace in the face of our deepest vulnerabilities. Addiction, once viewed through the narrow lens of moral failure, is reframed within the compassionate context of our death and new life in Jesus Christ. In this way, theology is not an academic exercise but a balm for the wounded soul, guiding us toward the mercy that transcends judgment and the grace that surpasses condemnation.

Throughout this theological odyssey, we've confronted the stark reality that addiction is not always conquered. Rather, it is often endured with a tenacious faith that clings to the promise of a God who walks with us in the valleys of despair.

The theological reflections in this book have invited us to redefine victory, urging us to shift our focus from eradicating the struggle to the strength found while enduring it. Recovery, we've come to understand, is not a finish line but an unceasing acknowledgment of our dependence on the sustaining grace of God.

Our exploration of biblical narratives has served as a lantern, illuminating the universal human experience of seeking an unattainable prize. The stories of the prodigal son and the bound man liberated by Christ's touch have become mirrors reflecting our yearning for restoration and deliverance. Through these narratives, we've witnessed the divine invitation to a feast of mercy, where shame is replaced by the compassionate vocabulary of grace.

As we draw this theological examination to its conclusion, we find ourselves standing at the intersection of surrender and redemption. The transformative power of community has been unveiled as an essential companion—a fellowship of fellow dead men walking, each wrestling with their own impossible prizes. In the sacramental nature of recovery, we've discovered a profound connection between the tangible elements of faith and the intangible grace that flows through them.

In this grace, we reach our conclusion and embrace the paradox that the pursuit of an impossible prize is not an exercise of futility but a testament to the transformative nature of God's Word when it grasps hold of us. Yet, we continue to grapple with the tension between the longing for satisfaction, security, and success and the humility required to acknowledge our dependence on God. It's a dance of surrender and strength, of acknowledging our weakness and finding enduring fortitude in the boundless love of the divine.

Much like the impossible prize itself, the journey is not neatly tied with a bow. It's an ongoing narrative, a continuous pilgrimage that beckons us to explore the depths of grace, resilience, and the ever-present mercy of God. In the conclusion of *The Impossible Prize*, we are left with the resounding truth that recovery is not a destination but a perpetual turning toward the divine, a daily recognition of our need for the God who meets us in broken places.

As we step away from these pages, may we carry with us the echoes of theological reflections, the whispers of biblical narratives, and the enduring truth that the impossible prize is not a distant goal but a present reality—a God who, amid our struggles, offers the unattainable gift of unfathomable love and inexhaustible grace.

ABOUT THE AUTHOR

*Donavon Riley is a father, husband, and Lutheran pastor currently living in a village at the edge of a great woods with his wife, five children, and their English Mastiff, Rachel. When he's not writing articles, poetry, or prayers inspired by early Anglo-Saxon Christianity, he can be found at one of two gyms training, teaching, or coaching mixed martial arts. He is also the author of the books **Crucifying Religion** and **The Withertongue Emails**. He is the co-host of the Banned Books podcast and host of The Warrior Priest podcast.*

More Best Sellers from

FIFTEEN-SEVENTEEN PUBLISHING

1517.

Find these titles
and more at 1517.org/**shop**

Never Go Another Day Without Hearing the Gospel of Jesus.

Visit **www.1517.org**
for free Gospel resources.